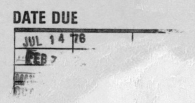

Perspectives on Justice

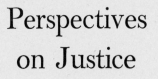

Perspectives
on Justice

Telford Taylor

Constance Baker Motley

James K. Feibleman

1973 ROSENTHAL LECTURES
Northwestern University School of Law

NORTHWESTERN UNIVERSITY PRESS
Evanston, Illinois

THE JULIUS ROSENTHAL FOUNDATION was established in 1926 to encourage preparation and publication of meritorious works of legal literature. Over the years the Rosenthal Lectures have been recognized as outstanding contributions to legal thought.

Julius Rosenthal (1827–1905), in whose honor the Foundation was established, was an eminent and beloved member of the Chicago Bar.

Copyright © 1975 by Northwestern University Press
Library of Congress Catalog Card Number: 74-14309
ISBN: 0-8101-0453-9

Telford Taylor is Professor of Law at Columbia University.

The Honorable Constance Baker Motley is United States District Judge for the Southern District of New York.

James K. Feibleman holds the W. R. Irby Chair as Professor of Philosophy at Tulane University.

Preface

IN PLANNING THE Julius Rosenthal Foundation Lectures for 1973, Northwestern's committee of faculty, students, and alumni sought to evoke conceptions and analyses of justice from multiple perspectives. Of special concern were the contrasting objectives, operations, and outputs of such central regulators of human behavior as the criminal justice system and the laws of war. We hoped also to learn more of how philosophy views the functions, dysfunctions, and anomalies of justice. Must justice wither when war erupts? Does the notion of "laws of war" mock the essential quest of justice for equitable resolution of conflict? In the administration of criminal justice, are there common standards for imposing sentences or engaging in plea bargaining that comport with the goal of "equal justice under law"? Or does unchanneled discretion that tolerates even whimsy dominate day-to-day practices of judicial officials? Does philosophy interpret, rationalize, or challenge the normative and empirical dimension of justice?

Emulating the format of the 1965 Rosenthal Lectures, when three distinguished speakers representing the disciplines of political science, law, and journalism presented their varying perspectives on the Supreme Court, we asked three renowned scholars from the realms of law teaching and practice, the judiciary, and philosophy to address themselves to the concept of justice from their respective personal and professional vantage points.

Professor Telford Taylor, who spoke on "The Concept of Justice and the Laws of War," has combined in his career extensive government service with an immensely creative life as lawyer, law professor, and author. He served as a colonel in Military Intelligence during World War II and subsequently became chief counsel of the U.S. Office of Military Government for the prosecution of war crimes. His books include *Sword and Swastika*, *Grand Inquest*, and *Nuremburg and Vietnam*.

The Honorable Constance Baker Motley spoke on "Criminal Law: 'Law and Order' and the Criminal Justice System." Her appointment as U.S. District Judge for the Southern District of New York by President

Lyndon Johnson in 1966 followed her distinguished public service as a member of the New York State Senate, President of the Borough of Manhattan, and human rights leader through the Legal Defense and Educational Fund of the NAACP.

James K. Feibleman presented the "Philosophical Perspectives on Justice" of a scholar renowned for three decades of inspired teaching at Tulane University, where he holds the W. R. Irby Professorship of Philosophy, and for his prolific and creative authorship in the many-faceted domains of philosophy, including *Ontology, Institutions of Society, Foundations of Empiricism*, and *Moral Strategy*.

We hope that the reader will find these lectures as informative and provocative as did the Northwestern community when Professor Taylor, Judge Motley, and Professor Feibleman delivered them.

VICTOR G. ROSENBLUM, *Chairman*
1973 Rosenthal Foundation Lectures

Contents

I

The Concept of Justice
and the Laws of War

Telford Taylor

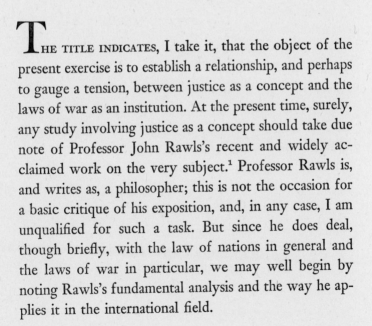

THE TITLE INDICATES, I take it, that the object of the present exercise is to establish a relationship, and perhaps to gauge a tension, between justice as a concept and the laws of war as an institution. At the present time, surely, any study involving justice as a concept should take due note of Professor John Rawls's recent and widely acclaimed work on the very subject.[1] Professor Rawls is, and writes as, a philosopher; this is not the occasion for a basic critique of his exposition, and, in any case, I am unqualified for such a task. But since he does deal, though briefly, with the law of nations in general and the laws of war in particular, we may well begin by noting Rawls's fundamental analysis and the way he applies it in the international field.

Now, as no doubt many of you know, the thrust of Rawls's work is to attack the logical sufficiency of utilitarianism and expound, as preferable, a form of the social-contract theory. It is a highly sophisticated presentation, and, I hardly need say, there is no nonsense about an actual meeting of prehistoric noble savages at which the social contract was formulated.

Rawls's projection of his theory is abstract: principles of justice should be deduced *as if* at a meeting of rational men in what he calls the "original position"—that is, without knowledge of one another's varying capacities, characteristics, and circumstances. This is what he calls "justice as *fairness*," which does not mean that justice *is* fairness but rather that its principles should be derived from an original position which is fair because all the formulators are on an identical footing.

The two basic principles of justice which he constructs from this original position are: (1) everyone has a clear right to the most extensive liberty compatible with similar liberty for others, and (2) social and economic inequalities are to be so arranged that they redound to everyone's advantage and that privileges are attached to positions open to all. The nub of his attack on utilitarianism is that rational men in the "original position" would not accept it: "Since each desires to protect his interest . . . no one has a reason to acquiesce in any enduring loss for himself in order to bring about a greater net balance of satisfaction. . . . Thus it seems that the principle of utilitarianism is incompatible with the conception of social cooperation among equals for mutual advantage." [2]

Insofar as Rawls is combating a quantitative approach to justice—quantitative, that is, in terms of population count—I cannot fault him. If utilitarianism means to justify subjecting a thousand souls to the tortures of Hades so that two thousand may revel on Mount Olympus, I cannot accept it. But surely that is a crude utilitarianism. In the "closed community" that Rawls postulates, the two thousand on Mount Olympus would be aware of what was going on below, and that would sour the nectar and spoil the ambrosia. Like my late and deeply lamented colleague, Wolfgang Friedmann, I am not convinced that Rawls's antithesis of social contract and utilitarianism is as basic as he thinks it is and am disposed to regard it as a difference "of emphasis rather than of fundamentals." [3]

But my real quarrel with Rawls lies not at the heart of his general thesis but rather with the manner with which he seeks to apply that thesis to international law. [4] He does this simply by transmuting his "original position" from a closed community of men, speaking for themselves, to a group of men "as representatives of different nations who must choose together the fundamental principles to adjudicate the conflicting claims among states." The groups so "represented" thus become "states," and these states are now assumed to develop the principles of interstate justice, in exactly the same fashion as individuals in the "original position."

As Rawls puts it: "Justice between states is determined by the principles that would be chosen in the original position so interpreted. . . . The national interest of a just state is defined by the principles of justice that have already been acknowledged." Among the international principles that would be thus chosen, he specifies "self-determination," the "right to self-defense against attack," the obligation to honor treaties, the right to pursue "a just cause in war," and the obligation to observe limits on the methods by which war may be waged. And he goes on to paint a rather idyllic picture of the way a "just" state "not moved by the desire for world power or national glory" would behave.[5]

Now, it goes almost without saying that this is very far from being an accurate description of the law of nations as we find it today,[6] but quite possibly Professor Rawls did not mean it for such. However that may be, I think that in the extrapolation of his "original position" to the international situation, he has overlooked his own postulates and made a false transference which has led him to an unsound concept of the law of nations.

To begin with, the "original position" on which he grounds his general thesis is conceived as "a closed system isolated from other societies."[7] The "joint act" of choosing principles is performed by everyone that the participants know to exist. But if they then become aware of other groups, why should we assume that they would choose "representatives" and deal with the others as separate states? By Rawls's hypothesis none of the members of any of the groups knows of any specific or variant circumstances or qualities differentiating one group from another. Since we are positing a hypothetical rather than an actual situation, considerations of distance, numbers, or other inconveniences are irrelevant. It seems much more logical to suppose that all groups known to one another would meet together to choose the basic principles of justice, rather than send "representatives."[8]

Once this were done, and the basic principles of justice chosen, of course they might then create either a single legislature or, aware of distance or other factors, might create several.[9] Be it one way or the other, the basic principles would have been chosen, not by representatives—i.e., governments—of the several groups, but by the people of all of them in one joint act, and the states as entities would not be the source of the principles of justice but would rather be subject to them. To me, this is the only logical projection internationally of Rawls's general theory, and he offers no reason for his abrupt departure from his own conception.

7

For the American constitutional lawyer, the issue is a familiar one. In 1819 Walter Jones, appearing for the State of Maryland in *McCulloch v. Maryland*, told the Supreme Court that the Constitution is "a compact between the states." [10] He was strongly answered from the other side by William Pinkney: "But the Constitution acts directly on the people, by means of powers mandated directly from the people . . . precisely as the state constitutions spring from the people. . . . The state sovereignties are not the authors of the Constitution of the United States." [11] And we all know Marshall's resolution of the issue so posed: "The government of the Union . . . is emphatically and truly a government of the people. In form and substance it emanates from them." [12] On all of this Abraham Lincoln placed the capstone with his exhortation at Gettysburg in behalf of our "government of the people, by the people, and for the people."

Lest you accuse me of committing Rawls's error of false transference, let me remind you that, in American constitutional law, questions of federalism, while not international, are in a limited but substantial sense intersovereign. And in any event, the view that the binding application of international law springs from the people, not from their governments, is anything but novel. It is, indeed, the view of the single authority on international law cited by Rawls. [13] The late J. L. Brierly, for a quarter of a century Chichele Professor of Law at Oxford University, after rejecting both the "natural right of states" and "consent of states" as the basis of obligation in the law of nations, concluded that the law of nations must stand on the same footing as law in general, without distinction between states and individuals.[14]

Rawls's view, it seems to me, also involves an anthropomorphic image of states, which he characterizes as "just" and "unjust" and to which he attributes motivations based on the same principles of justice that he derives for the governance of individuals.[15] As Brierly puts it, states are not "individuals writ large"; they are institutions through which individuals act. Furthermore, individuals acting through or for the state often reason very differently about justice than they do in their private capacities.

Finally, Rawls's idea that international principles of justice are to be determined by "representatives" of the several previously closed communities seems to me to lead to a system in which the principles are binding only on the states as entities and not on the individuals who compose them. To be sure, the national governments can make the international principles binding on their members, but then the individuals are bound by international law only as it is incorporated in domestic law. And if the national government fails to relay the obligation, what then? We are led back to the notion that international law binds states only and does not act directly on individuals. Although this view has had its exponents, it commands small support today; and it certainly is not where Professor Rawls meant to come out, since his discussion of "the justification of conscientious refusal"—i.e., civil disobedience—plainly postulates a right if not a duty to disobey national commands that contravene international principles of justice.[16]

To summarize, then, it is my view that the principles of justice in international law must be conceived as emanating from the same source as law in general. Governments are partial embodiments of those principles, but they are not the source. Nations are not the authors of the law of nations, and individuals cannot escape the binding obligation of international principles merely because their national governments have repudiated or are violating them. To be sure, there are requirements of international law that only a state can fulfill or reject. Only a state—in embryo or in maturity—can create a condition of war, just or unjust. But if the state acts contrary to the requirements of international law, responsibility attaches to the individuals who steered it into unlawful paths. That the question of sanctions is both difficult and unresolved does not detract from the responsibility; as Brierly observes, I think rightly, differences of enforcement as between international and domestic law are "organizational" rather than intrinsic.[17]

Those unsatisfied with these few pages written in the pursuit of logic may perhaps be persuaded by the volumes of history. During the era of the theologians, the supranational authority of the law of nations was acknowledged as virtually self-evident.[18] "If a subject be convinced of the injustice of a war, he ought not to serve in it, even on the command of his prince," wrote the great Spanish Dominican Francisco de Vitoria early in the sixteenth century; "subjects whose conscience is against the justice of a war may not engage in it, whether they be right or wrong."[19] Even in 1899, at the height of the nationalist approach to international polity, the sovereign parties to the Hague Convention with Respect to the Laws and Customs of War on Land referred, in the preamble, to the "principles of international law" not as their own creation but "as they result from the usages established between civilized nations, from the laws of humanity, and from the dictates of the public conscience." If more were needed, the postwar judgments of the Nuremberg and other tribunals, the basic principles of which were approved by the General Assembly of the United Nations, have, by the imposition of penal sanctions, confirmed the doctrine of individual responsibility under international law.

My effort so far has been to establish that the source of principles of justice must be the same internationally and domestically. I have made no effort to define the source itself, and I do not propose to do so. Whether it be conceived as contractual, utilitarian, or other would not, I believe, much affect the rest of what I have to say.

In the abstract, if mankind as a whole in Rawls's "original position" were to choose universal principles of justice, I have little doubt that reason would dictate the establishment of a single charter and government to enact and apply the laws in accord with the principles. But in historical fact, human society has been familial, tribal, and national and has evolved into discrete sovereign entities. The international principles of justice which can credibly be thought to have been "chosen" by mankind in general are narrowly limited by this circumstance.

Governments—in other words, men as representatives of nations—are inhibited in their rationality by the very fact of representation. A rational individual may perceive the benefits of concession and take the long view. But the representative man must reckon with his constituents. The corporate director is reluctant to be generous with the stockholders' money, for fear that they may not accept his argument that generosity will eventually redound to their advantage. The psychology of national groups, emotionally charged as it is by tradition and the symbols of patriotism, fosters governmental behavior vis-à-vis other nations that would be intolerable between individuals. A national leader's success is all too likely to be gauged not by his sensitivity to the developing needs of mankind but by immediate and spectacular "gains" for his country. Few indeed are the international principles which the people of a nation will acknowledge as binding when the result of their application appears seriously disadvantageous to them.

Justice is procedural as well as substantive, and the limits apply here even more sharply. The very idea that the individual is bound by a law of nations superior to domestic law creates a serious tension, for men live their lives in the medium of nationality. The domestic sanction for disobedience to local law is imminent, while the international sanction is at least remote, probably invisible, and generally nonexistent. Philosophically, of course, the validity of a principle of conduct may not depend on the availability of coercive force to ensure its observance. But rational men will certainly choose such principles much more cautiously and selectively if they know in advance that the means of their enforcement will be scanty at best.

With all this in mind, let us look at the principles of international justice which Rawls derived from his "original position" of national representatives and which consist of both rights and obligations. The rights of "self-determination" and of "self-defense against attack" and the obligation to honor treaties all seem to me credible as principles that rational men would choose, though of course difficult questions of application arise from all of them. The "right of a people to settle its own affairs without the intervention of foreign powers" is far more debatable: did the Third Reich have the "right" to exterminate German Jews free of foreign intervention? The Soviet Union to establish a Vorkuta? Or was it only that foreign intervention would have been either ineffective or productive of even worse evils? But these questions are only collaterally relevant to our present inquiry. Directly in point, however, are Rawls's declaration of the right of nations to wage war for "a just cause" and their obligation to refrain from "certain forms of violence" that are "inadmissible" even in a just war.[20]

We are thus brought, finally, to the nub of the exercise. Are the laws of war a legitimate embodiment of international principles of justice? Rawls's case for the affirmative is succinctly stated:

> The aim of war is a just peace, and therefore the means employed must not destroy the possibility of peace or encourage a contempt for human life that puts the safety of ourselves and of mankind in jeopardy. The conduct of war is to be constrained and adjusted to this end. The representatives of states would recognize that their national interest, as seen

from the original position, is best served by acknowl-
edging these limits on the means of war.[21]

In a monograph on the laws of war as applied to the
fighting in Vietnam which I wrote in 1970, I did not
explicitly discuss whether the laws of war were compatible with the concept of justice, but I certainly implied that they were.[22] My view did not escape unchal-
lenged in the book reviews, and I found it noteworthy
that it appeared especially uncongenial to those wedded
to nonlegal disciplines, such as philosophy and lin-
guistics.[23]

Assessment of the laws of war requires, I believe, a
brief preliminary scrutiny of war itself. In a universal
"original position," I am sure that rational men would
have chosen principles and organizations in a unity that
would have eliminated the possibility of international
warfare. But the story of mankind has been in large part
a military story, and this has led to attempts to distinguish among wars on principled grounds. The theologians spoke of "just" and "unjust" wars, a distinction
which, in the present century, has largely given way to
one between "aggressive" and "defensive" wars. Rawls
states that his "principles" will "define when a nation
has a just cause in war," presumably referring to self-
determination, self-defense, and treaty observance. But
I find these criteria far from sufficient, especially since

circumstances may well (and do) arise in which they cancel each other out.

The unfortunate fact is that while many criteria, plausible or even valid considered by themselves, have been advanced for distinguishing just from unjust wars, there are too many cases where there is much to be said on both sides. A war may well be unjust on both sides. Sometimes, as in the case of Hitler's aggressions, the evidence may be clear enough, but that is the exceptional case. If Egypt closes off Israel's access to the Red Sea and Israel retaliates by occupying the Sinai Peninsula, on which side is the war "just"? I know that many people think the answer perfectly plain, but they are sharply divided on what is the correct answer.

These difficulties make more attractive a conclusion that there is simply no place for war in the concept of justice, any more than there is a place for self-help by force as the means of settling domestic disputes. Quakers and others have so contended with good show of reason and faith. But even those who are not total pacifists have in recent years voiced variants of this view, usually under the stimulus of revulsion at our military involvement in Vietnam. Professor Richard Wasserstrom, for example, has criticized "preoccupation with the laws of war" on the ground that it tends "to divert us from the question of why it is wrong for us to be fighting there at all." [24]

This, of course, is an argument in the area of effective political tactics rather than conceptual jurisprudence, and Wasserstrom does not go so far as to deny the intrinsic validity of the laws of war as a general institution. But there are those who do.

Sometimes the point is made in pragmatic terms: that "war at best is Hell, and that true humanity lies in exaggerating that Hell to such an extent as to make it unendurable." [25] On this theory the soldiers of Genghis Khan and Wallenstein did us a favor by behaving as they are said to have, and the massacre of Jews and Poles in Eastern Europe during the Second World War were admirable steps in a good cause. The trouble with the theory is that mankind's capacity to "endure" such things and come back for more is far greater than the sponsors of this kill-and-cure technique have realized.

But the argument is also advanced in jural terms: that the coupling of law and war is an "unnatural" one; that to have laws about war necessarily involves the recognition of war itself as "legal," whereas we should rather start with the proposition that war is the antithesis of law. [26]

This view is what the French would call *sympathique*, and it is especially appealing today, in the welter of Vietnam horrors and nuclear menace. But I do not believe that it is sound. It may be answered on two levels —the historical and the pragmatic—and for the first I can do no better than to quote, once more, Professor Brierly:

Casual unorganized mobs can engage in a brawl or a riot, but they cannot wage a war. War has always been a formal procedure, requiring, even in its most primitive form, some degree of social organization in the parties engaging in it. Something like a declaration of war, to mark the transition from a state of peace to one of war; something like a treaty of peace, to mark that from war to peace; some rudiments of understanding between the parties as to some of the incidents of war, for example, a rule of respect for a herald or a flag of truce; war cannot be stripped of formal and organized concomitants such as these without ceasing to be war. In fact, it is the simple truth, though it may sound a paradox, to say that an admixture of law is what differentiates war from mere fighting, and that a rudimentary law of war is coeval with war itself.[27]

I accept this lesson of history, but I think there is a deeper answer to the point at issue. We have the record of human experience, and we know that war has been a more or less constant historical phenomenon. Despite the terrible teaching of two world wars in less than half a century, despite the pacts for the renunciation of war, despite the judicial condemnation of aggressive war at Nuremberg and Tokyo, despite the United Nations and its Charter, there have been one or more wars of sub-

stantial proportions going on constantly since the end of
the Second World War. I think we know the reason
why: it is because other means of settling the issues in
international and revolutionary disputes have not been
acceptable to the parties. Precisely for the same reason—
that the government's decision-making and dispute-
settling mechanisms work in ways that large sections of
the population find intolerable—we are experiencing a
period of increased domestic disorder and violence—as
witness Watts and Wounded Knee.

Denunciation of the evil will not cure us of war any
more than of cancer. I think we must start with recognition of the fact that the pacific settlement of disputes
of international or revolutionary magnitude is a technique which men have not been able to master other
than occasionally, that the present prospects of improvement are at best speculative, and that war is likely to remain a part of the human condition for a long time to
come.

This circumstance may be grievous, as all violence and
death are grievous, but it is not new; it has been a mark
of the human condition since the beginning. By no
means do I suggest abandonment of efforts to erase it,
but considerations of prudence, humanity, and, I now
add, *justice* dictate that we also do everything possible
to mitigate its evils. The laws of war, I say, do not necessarily acknowledge the validity, let alone the desirability,

of war; rather they recognize war as a recurrent condition of men, to the alleviation of which law may contribute.

The questions then remain: what are the principles of justice which should govern the substantive content of the laws of war, and do the laws of war in their present form sufficiently correspond to those principles to deserve their designation as "laws"? Obviously, the particulars which might be discovered under these general issues are legion. I shall confine myself to dealing with the three that seem to me most important, and I shall take them in what appears to me as an ascending order of difficulty.

The first question is whether there is a relation between the laws of war, as they apply to a belligerent nation, and the "justness" or "unjustness" of the war that the nation is conducting. On this point I must once more mention Rawls, whose answer is categorically affirmative: "Where a country's right to war is questionable and uncertain, the constraints on the means it can use are all the more severe. Acts permissible in a war of legitimate self-defense, when these are necessary, may be flatly excluded in a more doubtful situation." [23]

Rawls states the principle thus baldly, without supporting explanation of any kind. I think he is wrong, but I think it is easy to infer what he has in mind. A man or woman resisting a mugger is not expected to observe the Marquess of Queensberry rules. The onlooker is so outraged by the attack that *anything* the victim does to frustrate and punish the miscreant appears justifiable and gratifies the desire to see him get his just deserts.

However, we are not discussing a street encounter but a war. In the history and judicial precedents of the laws of war there is no basis for Rawls's view, though in an excess of prosecutorial zeal it was once put forward under my authority at Nuremberg, where it received short shrift in the Tribunal's judgment.[29] And in our very first official codification of the laws of war—the famous General Orders No. 100 of 1863, commonly known as the Lieber Code—it was made quite explicit that the laws are equally binding on a government attacked by "a wanton and unjust assailant" and on the aggressor government.[30]

Is there any reason to change this settled rule in favor of Rawls's view? It appears to me that pragmatic considerations speak decisively to the contrary. We must remember that observance of the laws of war, even more than observance of domestic criminal law, depends on voluntary compliance rather than enforcement by police sanctions. Is it conceivable that, in wartime, either (or any) party to the conflict would admit his cause to be unjust or his enemy's just? Certainly not; and if we were to adopt any such principle as Rawls advocates, the inevitable result would be that all belligerents would claim for themselves the greater latitude of the injured party. I can think of nothing better calculated to erode the scope and effect of the laws of war or more in conflict with their governing purpose of mitigating war's consequences.[31]

The second, and, to my mind, much more complex question, concerns the substantive purposes which the laws of war should seek to achieve, and it embraces primarily the concepts of "military necessity," "reciprocity," and "proportionality." It is in these areas that my views have proved especially uncongenial to my nonlegal critics.[32] I have taken the positions that, generally speaking, the laws of war can effectively prohibit only actions which are not reasonably related to the successful conduct of hostilities or which do not yield military advantage reasonably proportional to the damage they inflict and that, consequently, the specific content of the laws of war will fluctuate in reaction to changing military techniques and circumstances. The critics have replied that if the laws of war can accomplish no more than this, they are not worth much attention, and that if they deserve the name of "law" they must be categorical and permanent prohibitions, superior to the

changing pressures of military factors. In Professor
Wasserstrom's words:

> . . . if Taylor has outlined with reasonable accuracy
> the rules and principles which determine what is and
> is not a war crime—then he has demonstrated, I be-
> lieve, that the laws of war are not of much importance
> morally and that they are not morally admirable in-
> ventions.[33]

Much as I sympathize with the feelings that prompt
such criticism, I suggest that its author should be reminded that "the matter of legal science is not an ideal
result of ethical or political analysis; it is the result of
human nature and history." [34] Once again, Brierly has
stated the limiting principle most succinctly:

> Nothing can alter the inexorable fact that the limits
> of an effective law of war are set by war itself, and
> that they are narrow. . . . Nothing but a State's
> determination to make its will prevail at all costs over
> the will of its opponent can make war worth while; if
> States are prepared to compromise on that issue there
> will be no war. . . . The preamble to the Hague
> Regulations states that their authors were "inspired by
> the desire to diminish the evils of war, *as far as mili-
> tary requirements permit*," and however much we
> may resent this saving clause, the laws of war cannot

escape from it. If they could, it would mean that men were prepared to make victory their secondary, and some other end their primary, purpose in war, and if that were so, they would not go to war at all.[35]

The limitation must be accepted; but while the consequence is of course restrictive of the scope of the laws of war, I do not think it is disastrous to either their practical importance or moral value. It is only necessary to reflect on what has been going on in Vietnam during the past few weeks. Despite the rain of destruction and death from our bombers over North Vietnam, the crew members who had to take to their parachutes were treated as prisoners of war, as the laws of war require, and are now alive and being repatriated. Despite the ferocious internecine hatreds and hostilities that have rent that unhappy country, and despite the stories of "tiger cage" prisons at Con Son, Saigon and the Viet Cong *are* exchanging their prisoners of war.

Furthermore, the limitation by military necessity is not at all so narrow as some of its critics suppose, such as Wasserstrom, who declares that "there is something genuinely odious about a code of behavior that says: if there is a conflict between the attainment of an important military objective and one or more of the prohibitions of the laws of war, it is the prohibitions that properly are to give way." [36] Insofar as he suggests that a commander confronted with the opportunity for gaining a local military advantage by disregarding a law of war is entitled to disregard it, this is wholly inaccurate. The laws of war are not susceptible to violation on any such occasional basis. Rather, it is only when changing techniques have rendered a rule obsolete for all belligerents that it loses its binding character, as in the case of the 1936 London Naval Treaty restrictions on submarine warfare, which no belligerent could observe after the advent of long-range aircraft, radar, sonar, and convoys.[37] "Military necessity" is to be taken in the long-term general sense rather than with reference to transitory, particular situations.

It is also important to distinguish between situations in which a rule of war becomes obsolete for reasons that affect all belligerents and those in which, on both sides of a conflict, rules are violated which are still viable for warfare generally. Barbaric practices of torture, mutilation, and wanton massacre may be and have been resorted to on both sides of particular conflicts, but this would in no way operate to nullify the prohibitory laws of war.[38]

But mutual violation may well relate to the selection of a tribunal to conduct war-crimes trials. Principles of justice cannot be formulated without considering the means available for enforcement, and my own attitude on these questions is profoundly affected by the lack of any neutral international tribunal of general criminal jurisdiction. The Nuremberg and Tokyo tribunals were international but not neutral and had jurisdiction only over the nationals of the defeated countries. And apart from those two experiences, war-crimes tribunals have been nationally created and have tried either nationals of their own countries or captured enemies.[39] Before all such tribunals, the *tu quoque* principle is obviously relevant. For the enforcing nation to punish violators of laws which the enforcer has likewise transgressed would be shocking to the sense of fairness and would undermine rather than support international principles of justice.

I am very far from suggesting that the shifting character of the laws of war is not a complicating and, indeed, a weakening factor. Given an international criminal jurisdiction, a more rigorous and stable system of rules might well be feasible. Until such a jurisdiction is created, however, I can see nothing in these limitations that renders the laws of war incompatible with principles of justice.

I now come to the third and last of these issues, and the one with respect to which I find it most difficult—indeed impossible—to justify the laws of war in their present condition. Discussing the requirement that a "just" legal system shall operate with substantial regularity and equality, John Rawls writes: "If deviations from justice as regularity are too pervasive, a serious question may arise whether a system of law exists as opposed to a collection of particular orders designed to advance the interests of a dictator or the ideal of a benevolent despot." [40] In the structure of the laws of war we have no dictators or despots in the picture, but we are far from having the generality or equality of either scope or enforcement which Rawls's entirely sound principle would require.

Let us first consider their shortcomings of scope. In the Hague and Geneva conventions we have an extensive, though not comprehensive, and a reasonably systematic collection of rules governing warfare on land. [41] There are many gaps, and the rules do not address problems of individual responsibility, legal procedure, or sanctions; but at least there is a framework and a considerable number of particulars.

But there is nothing comparable relating to war at sea. The 1864 Red Cross Convention was adapted and made applicable to maritime warfare in 1899 by the Third Hague Convention; a series of conventions relating to merchant shipping, submarine mines, neutral rights, and prizes were signed at The Hague in 1907; blockade and contraband were dealt with in the London Naval Declarations of 1909; the soon-to-be-proved-abortive rules of submarine warfare were signed at

London in 1936. There is, however, no generality of scope comparable to that obtaining in the law of land warfare.

Much more serious, considering the course of events, is the paucity of rules governing aerial warfare, and particularly aerial bombardment of enemy territory. The Red Cross conventions are applicable to air-force operations, as are the provisions of the 1949 Geneva Convention for the protection of civilians in occupied territory. Article XXV of the 1899 Hague Convention on land warfare, prohibiting the bombardment of undefended localities, is presumably applicable to aerial bombardment, and some of the other provisions of that treaty may also be considered to limit aerial operations. But there is no general code and nothing that clearly applies to massive aerial bombardments such as those of the Second World War or such as our Air Force recently carried out over North Vietnam.[42] And there was nothing decided at Nuremberg or any of the other post–Second World War war-crimes trials that sheds any judicial light on these questions.

Now, there are historical and political circumstances that explain how and why this unbalanced situation has come about. But the consequence of the imbalance is questions such as: "Is there any significant difference between killing a babe-in-arms by a bomb dropped from a high-flying aircraft, or by an infantryman's point-blank gunfire?" There are answers to this question, which I myself have given and which I believe to be not insubstantial.[43] But it is apparent that they fall short of satisfying many people and that this wide gulf between the laws of war on the ground as compared to the air is working strongly to discredit the entire fabric of *lex belli*. There is, furthermore, a growing belief that aerial bombardment has become so dominant an ingredient of warfare that its exclusion from coverage by the laws of war leaves *Hamlet* without Hamlet.

Rules for the governance of air warfare were drafted at The Hague in 1922–23 but were never adopted by the participating governments.[44] For reasons which have not been much explored, public opinion during the years between the two world wars settled into a fatalistic acceptance that future wars between the great powers would surely involve urban holocausts produced by bomber aircraft. So firm was this belief that, when such attacks failed to materialize during the first months of the Second World War, people spoke of the "phony war." Soon, of course, their expectations were fulfilled only too completely, though aerial bombardment proved far less effective in a military sense than its proponents had expected.

Now, as I have said, there are historical reasons for the systemization of the laws of land warfare as compared to war on the sea and in the air. The laws of war are only in part a response to humanitarian considerations. They respond also to the military need for discipline and to the desire of the commercial world that civilian life be interrupted by war as little as possible.[45] Discipline is easier to maintain on shipboard than in the field, and naval operations usually impinge on civilian life less than land campaigns. The laws of war were codified before the air became a major area of warfare; and, when it did, the great powers, who alone were able to make full use of it, did not agree on limitations.

But half a century has now elapsed since the abortive efforts of 1922–23. Air power has indeed proved a potent weapon; but the evidence from the Second World War, during which we and our allies eventually achieved decisive air superiority, and from Korea and Vietnam, where we have had it from start to finish, has been that massive bombardment of cities and towns is often counterproductive in a military sense. I think that today there is a possible basis for the development of laws of air warfare. And unless progress in that direction is made, I fear that the failure may make the laws of land warfare seem increasingly bizarre and anachronistic and that we will indeed find, in Rawls's words, that the "deviations from justice as regularity" are so great as to lead to their gradual extinction.

The other respect in which the laws of war fall lamentably, perhaps fatally, short of meeting the requirements of justice is with respect to the institutions and procedures available for the trial of war-crimes charges. The Nuremberg and Tokyo experience with international tribunals remains, so far, unique; and even these, as I have already said, were juridically flawed in that the courts had jurisdiction only over nationals of the defeated countries and were established and staffed by the victorious powers. Given the circumstances of the time, in my opinion, these shortcomings would have been exceedingly difficult if not impossible to rectify, but it would be most undesirable for them to be repeated.

From the beginnings of military judicial institutions, it appears to have been assumed that the laws of war would be enforced by court-martial proceedings against captive enemy defendants or against the trying country's own nationals. Neither method has proved at all adequate. Except in the rare event of total victory and occupation of the defeated country, trial of one's adversaries will depend upon the chancy factor of capture and will generally be limited to low-ranking combatants. Tribunals trying enemy nationals may succumb to hate or the desire for vengeance or may lean over backward to avoid those dangers. No matter how fairly conducted, such trials will always be subject to the stigma of "victor's justice."

War-crimes trials of one's own nationals have proved at least equally unsatisfactory, though for other reasons.

They have not worked so badly for noncombat crimes; robberies, rapes, and other assaults against civilians in occupied territory can be effectively dealt with by courts-martial and, in a well-disciplined army, present no great problem. But the matter is of quite another nature in the case of combat-related crimes like the Son My killings; and the difficulties may not inaptly be compared to those which are encountered in connection with domestic police brutality, except that the problems in the military setting are even more obstinate of solution.

Soldiers in combat are, like policemen—but far more so—committed to unpleasant and dangerous duties that should and do breed a strong *esprit de corps*. The tasks are also such as to arouse, in many of them, deep feelings of mission: protection of the public from crime, protection of the nation from foreign enemies. It goes hard with men so circumstanced to see one of their number punished for acting overzealously in the discharge of his duties. And so, when military men sit in judgment on their comrades-in-arms, their frequent reaction is to join hands in defense of those accused and of the reputation of their service.

So far as I know, the Philippine insurrection following the Spanish-American War was the first occasion on which the Army brought charges based on the laws of war against its own officers. Brigadier General Jacob H.

Smith was found to have sent a marine detachment into battle under orders to take no prisoners and to have stated: "I wish you to kill and burn. The more you kill and burn, the better you will please me." He was "admonished," and President Theodore Roosevelt ordered him to be retired from the service. First Lieutenant Preston Brown was found guilty of manslaughter for killing without cause a Filipino who had been apprehended; the court-martial sentenced Brown to dismissal and five years' imprisonment, but President Roosevelt set aside the sentence, fined him half a month's pay, and dropped him thirty files on the rank list.[46]

Twenty years later, under strong Allied pressure, the German government tried a handful of officers and men for war crimes committed during the First World War. The American experience was repeated; there were a few convictions, but the sentences were ridiculously light.[47]

However, we need not go so far into the past. The details of the Son My killings in March, 1968, were abundantly proved by photographs and admissions of the participants. Many officers and men were implicated both before and after the fact. One man only was convicted for his share in the episode, and that man— Lieutenant William Calley—has not yet spent more than a few hours in jail.[48]

However, these shabby records in America and

Germany shine by comparison with the Congo, Nigeria-Biafra, and Indonesia. The more recent Pakistan-Bangladesh fighting has left a particularly discouraging situation. India has been holding some 90,000 Pakistani soldiers and will not repatriate them because Bangladesh says there are war criminals among the prisoners—which no doubt is true. But does anyone believe that either Pakistan or Bangladesh would enforce the laws of war against its own troops? Would war-crimes trials of Pakistani soldiers by Bangladesh tribunals be satisfactory to anyone's sense of justice? Furthermore, it is probably a violation of the laws of war for India to continue to hold these prisoners, against whom no specific charges have yet been laid. The only possible solution consistent with justice is some sort of international or at least neutral tribunal; but no such step appears to be in prospect, and very likely the situation will persist in deadlock and eventually dissolve into one more instance of the laws of war being honored in their breach.[49]

We have our own smaller but vexing immediate dilemma. What should be done about Lieutenant Calley, now that it is plain that nothing will be done judicially about anyone else? For myself, I can think of no principle of justice that would now be served by imprisoning Calley. He does not need to be confined as dangerous. Retribution visited on one badly trained and unstable lieutenant is hardly divine. Far from serving as a deterrent, his punishment will merely underline the unpunished culpability of the many who have gotten off scot free. Certainly he should not be pardoned; but in my view there is much to be said for commutation, not on the basis of minimizing his guilt but with frank acknowledgment that the Army's judicial machinery wholly failed to cope with the challenge of the My Lai killings and that it would be irrational and indeed offensive to punish one for the guilt of many.

Despite my profound distress at these shortcomings of scope and application from which the laws of war suffer, I am not proposing their abandonment but their strengthening. If justice is more than an abstract concept, it must grapple with and not give way to injustice and irrationality.

But the laws of war must not be allowed to stagnate, or they will indeed come to be not worth the keeping. For the most part they are based on ideas that antedate the First World War; they were updated in part in 1949, but that is already a quarter of a century in the past. It is high time for a new effort and for new concepts that will bring aerial warfare more fully within the scope of the laws of war and establish a judicial structure and general jurisdiction for their enforcement. The concept of justice, as I view it, requires of us no less than these things.

II

Criminal Law: "Law and Order" and the Criminal Justice System

Constance Baker Motley

THE SHARP INCREASE in drug-related crimes on the streets of our cities in the past few years has made the phrase "law and order" a household refrain. Every candidate running for public office promises to curb "street crime" [1] by restoring "law and order" in the community. To most of these public office seekers, as well as those already in office, the key to such restoration is greatly increased prison terms—including life sentences—for those involved in the illegal sale of narcotics and for those users of illegal narcotics who commit violent crimes. And the crux of these harsh new proposals is that such prison terms should be mandatory. In addition, these proposals would deny persons convicted of narcotics offenses the usual opportunity for parole.[2] Some state legislative proposals have gone so far as to prohibit plea bargaining in such cases.[3] In short, retribution and deterrence—a theory of severe mandatory punishment for law violators, as opposed to any other theory or program for curbing the sale of drugs and for decreasing drug-related crimes—have seized the day.

The only certain consequence of this oversimplified approach to a multifaceted problem is that the judge alone, of all those involved in the administration of criminal justice, would be entirely stripped of his or her discretion in dealing with narcotics sellers and narcotics-related offenders.[4] A bar to plea bargaining would circumscribe the prosecutor's discretion in this one area. The remainder of the prosecutor's broad discretion, as well as the discretion of all other principals in the criminal justice system—the police, the jury, the jailer— would remain intact. The prohibition against parole would mean that the parole board stage of the criminal justice process would be completely eliminated with respect to narcotics crimes. And all other crimes, except those few carrying mandatory penalties, would remain subject to a wide, largely unrestrained discretion which the law reposes in the prosecutor, the trial judge, and the parole board.[5] In other words, there is another, perhaps even more significant, "law and order" problem in our system of criminal justice of which the public is not so aware. Needless to say, this is a problem which deserves as much attention, if not more, than crime in the streets. For those who have been all the way through our criminal justice system, including prison, the lawlessness of the system must be a major contributing factor to their inability to accept lawful conduct as a meaningful alternative way of life.[6]

Our criminal justice system, from beginning to end, lacks "law and order" to a substantial degree. As noted before, officials at each critical stage of the criminal justice process have and exercise discretion. Too often it is a wide, largely uncontrolled discretion or one that is inadequately guided.[7] Current proposals relating to the narcotics epidemic mindlessly seek to remove or control the discretion of only certain officials in this limited area,[8] whereas the real need today is for the development of clearly articulated standards—standards that will more effectively control, rather than abolish, the exercise of discretion by all of the officials to whom society has delegated the authority to determine whether an individual shall be deprived of his or her liberty.

My plan is to examine first the various stages in our criminal justice system with a view toward elucidating the lack of adequate standards for guiding the exercise of discretion by officials functioning at various stages of our criminal justice process. Then I shall present one view as to how more law and order may be brought to bear on the sentencing phase of the criminal justice process, the stage with which I am most familiar.

The Six Stages of the Criminal Justice Process

It is now a criminal justice axiom that very, very few persons who actually violate the law are caught, still fewer are actually arrested, and even fewer are prosecuted and convicted. Thus, a minute percentage of all those guilty of some infraction of the law are actually imprisoned.[9] But for those who are, the criminal justice system can be fairly divided into six parts: arrest, indictment, trial, sentence, prison, and then parole.

So-called street crime today takes many forms: there is the teenage pocketbook snatcher, the mugger, the addict with a knife, the small narcotics pusher, the addict pusher, the small soft-drug pusher, the addict who steals social security and welfare checks from hallway mailboxes, as well as the major narcotics and soft-drug pushers. Generally speaking, it is expected that the policemen on the beat will arrest these and other street criminals. These are the offenders against whom the public's rage is presently directed. The fact that hundreds of millions of dollars' worth of securities have been and are being stolen, that securities frauds now are astronomical, that the market may be flooded with dangerous medical drugs and adulterated foods, that consumer frauds may be "out of sight," and that government at every level may be losing the battle against corruption has not generated nearly so much rage. We do not hear, for example, any proposals for the imposition of severe mandatory minimum prison terms upon those convicted of involvement in a two-hundred-million-dollar securities fraud. Consequently, for those who are involved in the administration of justice, the reality is that the present harsh proposals are designed to deal with only one segment of the criminal society. And the full force of this new criminal justice mandate will come to bear only on those few who are unlucky enough to be arrested, prosecuted, and convicted.

As previously mentioned, these new proposals for severe mandatory minimum prison sentences will completely strip discretion only from the judge, who has the duty to impose sentence. Of course, if the proposed "no parole" provisions are also enacted into law, the parole board will also lose its discretion, in the sense that persons convicted on these terms will not be eligible for parole. The elimination of plea bargaining will deprive the prosecutor of only a part of his wide discretion. But all other principals in the criminal justice process will emerge with their discretion intact; they will, nevertheless, be greatly influenced in exercising this discretion by the existence of such severe mandatory penalties.

Consider the policeman on the beat, who must make street arrests of narcotics pushers, large and small. Unless the officer actually witnesses the commission of the crime, he will be acting in many instances upon information supplied to him by informers. On the basis of the information he receives, the officer has the discretionary power to arrest and to conduct a limited search incident to an arrest.[10] The officer is told that he may make an arrest only if he has "probable cause" to believe that a crime has been or is being committed.

In *United States v. Harris*[11] the "Burger Court" considered for the first time what the new Chief Justice called "the recurring question of what showing is constitutionally necessary to satisfy a magistrate that there is a substantial basis for crediting the report of an informant known to the police, but not identified to the magistrate, who purports to relate his personal knowledge of criminal activity."[12]

The sufficiency of the affidavit before the magistrate in that case was upheld 5 to 4, with no majority opinion. Since the same standards are applied to determine whether a police officer had "probable cause" to make a street arrest in the first place and a search incident thereto, it must be said of the Court's opinion in *Harris* that police officers, as well as the lower courts, are presently without a Supreme Court opinion setting forth clearly defined guidelines for crediting the information of an informer. As a result, the police will often be wrong in making or not making an arrest. In the former event, the policeman's basis for arrest is reviewable by the judge. In the latter event, it is not.

When a policeman fails to make an arrest he should have made, it can be said that he improperly exercised his discretion in favor of an accused person and against the interests of society. In the former case, where an improper arrest is made, it can be said that he exercised his discretion against the interests of both the accused and society. The individual will have a record of arrest. Society's interests are clearly not served by having persons improperly arrested. However, in both cases it can be said that the officer's faulty actions stemmed from the fact that he was inadequately guided in exercising his discretion. In both cases it is possible that one for whom the severe penalties were intended will have escaped.

Those involved in law enforcement have long recognized that even when certain crimes have been committed in a police officer's presence he sometimes exercises an assumed official discretion not to arrest.[13] The juvenile or young teen-ager who puts a brick through a suburban school window may be taken home by the police to his parents and punished by school or family. The ghetto child whose family cannot afford to pay to repair a similarly broken school window is more likely to receive the punishment of a juvenile or youth court. From that policeman's point of view, the suburban child may be a troublemaker, the ghetto teen-ager a juvenile delinquent. It may be a good thing for a policeman to have such discretion, but who has attempted to guide him in its exercise? A policeman is obviously more tempted to assume a discretion if the youngster will be facing a severe mandatory minimum sentence for the offense committed in the officer's presence.

The exercise of an inadequately guided discretion in effecting arrests is much more common at the local than at the federal level. The reason for this is the difference in the types of crimes that are prosecuted within each area. City policemen must deal with street crime and family offenses, where on-the-spot decisions are the rule.[14] In the federal system, most prosecutions are the result of intensive investigations by administrative agencies, such as the SEC, and law-enforcement agencies, like the FBI. Therefore, it is often agency personnel who exercise discretion in determining, after investigation, which cases are to be referred for possible criminal prosecution to the United States Attorney. Federal narcotics arrests generally follow investigation and surveillance of the accused by Special Agents of the Bureau of Narcotics and Dangerous Drugs (BNDD) to whom the contraband is sold. Because limitations of staff and money make wide-scale prosecution of offenders impractical, administrative agencies, as well as the BNDD and FBI, tend to focus on what are considered "key" or "strategic" cases or those involving the most notorious or dangerous law violators. The boundary between a "key" case and a "not-so-key" case is obviously a very subjective matter.

The fact that a person has been properly arrested or charged with a crime does not mean that he will be prosecuted. A prosecutor has wide discretion in deciding, in every category of crime, who will be prosecuted and who will not. The average prosecutor's favorite discretionary device for securing convictions in narcotics cases, as in other types of criminal cases, is to use an arrestee as an informant in exchange for a promise that the arrestee will not be prosecuted, at least not for the crime with which he has been charged. Federal and state narcotics agents who make arrests often use this discretionary device. Another device is to name the arrestee as a coconspirator but not a defendant in the indictment. The coconspirator, as everyone in law enforcement knows, is the one who is going to get everyone else convicted by testifying for the government.

Recently the head of the Criminal Division in the office of the United States Attorney for the Southern District of New York issued a memorandum to all assistant United States attorneys in that office stating that government attorneys have the discretion to permit a drug addict to enter the Treatment Alternative to Street Crime (TASC) program.[15] The memorandum also describes the procedure to be followed with respect to an addict admitted to the program. If, having been admitted to the treatment program, he is found in "satisfactory status" after a year, the complaint against him is to be dismissed; if, on the other hand, a defendant violates any of the conditions of his release, he is to be rearraigned. Such deferred prosecutions apply to all narcotics addicts.

Deferred prosecutions have long been afforded juveniles arrested for any federal law violation. The *Probation Manual* issued by the Administrative Office of the United States Courts sets forth the deferred-prosecution plan with respect to juveniles.[16] The plan permits the government attorney to defer prosecution of a "carefully selected" juvenile and place him under the informal supervision of a probation officer for a definite period of time. The Judicial Conference has said that the philosophy underlying the plan of deferred prosecution

is based on the belief that very often it is wiser not to prosecute juveniles at all, even as juvenile delinquents; that in many instances, offenders are capable of correction without prosecution; and that if prior to trial and conviction such juveniles are placed under supervision, prosecution becomes unnecessary. . . . By such a procedure, the juvenile is not stigmatized by a court record of any kind.[17]

The Judicial Conference report found a patent flaw in the deferred-prosecution approach. The plan was not codified and, as a result, allowed prosecutors wide discretion in determining when to initiate a deferred-prosecution procedure.[18]

To quote a 1967 Presidential Commission's Task Force Report on prosecutors:

[T]he system for making the charge decision remains generally inadequate. Prosecutors act without the benefit of direction or guidelines from either the legislature or higher levels of administration; their decisions are almost entirely free from judicial supervision. Decisions are to a great extent fortuitous because they are made on inadequate information about the offense, the offender, and the alternatives [to prosecution of the offender which are] available. . . . Often cases are prosecuted that should not be. Often offenders in need of treatment, supervision, or discipline are set free without being referred to appropriate community agencies or followed up in any way.[19]

Thus, the arrest of a suspect and the decision to prosecute him are the first points of the criminal process where authority is exercised largely without rules. This same undisciplined exercise of authority continues after prosecution of the accused begins. He remains subject to it until his final release from the criminal justice system.

After a defendant is arrested and charged with a crime, a determination is made as to whether he shall be released on bail pending trial. Here again some official's unguided or inadequately guided discretion takes hold. Even under the present federal Bail Reform Act,[20] wide discretion still resides in the magistrate or the trial judge in determining what conditions of release are to be set for a defendant who is not released on his own recognizance or on an unsecured appearance bond. The judicial officer may consider such things as the defendant's family ties, his character and mental condition, and his length of residence in the community.[21]

Recent New York state proposals have included a provision that, with respect to persons arrested and charged with narcotics law violations or the use of violence while under the influence of drugs, there shall be no plea bargaining or very strictly limited plea bargaining.[22] If such provisions should become law, they would indeed "cramp" the prosecutor's "style" for securing many convictions.

In the plea bargaining process, which ends in the conviction of the defendant, there are no rules or standards to govern the prosecutor's conduct other than the tactical and strategic considerations which surround the performance of any difficult job.[23] In other words, the prosecutor's discretion in negotiating plea bargains is virtually without limit. How this discretion is exercised may depend on the nature of the evidence and the time constraints on the prosecutor's office rather than on considerations of justice and fairness.

Two other important dimensions of the plea bargaining process are worthy of attention. First, successful plea bargaining by-passes the trial process altogether. The courts, more out of necessity than conviction, countenance the waiver of basic constitutional rights by pleading defendants. The effect which no trial has upon sentencing can be tremendous. During the course of a trial, the government's proof as to all charges is revealed to court and jury, the nature and extent of the defendant's involvement are usually fully disclosed, and the seriousness of the crime or crimes committed by the defendant is put in perspective. In the case of a guilty plea, on the contrary, the judge usually hears only a brief summary of the prosecutor's version of the facts.

The other important dimension of the plea bargaining process is its effect as a sentencing decision. Generally it is thought, and legislatures have so provided, that sentences should be imposed by judges.[24] However, in most plea bargaining arrangements, prosecutors exercise this function,[25] since the reduction of charges, which is the quid pro quo for the defendant's plea of guilty, often effects a reduction in the maximum penalty which the judge may subsequently impose. In the Federal District Court for the Southern District of New York, this is generally the only effect of the plea bargain, since prosecutors are not given an opportunity to make specific sentencing recommendations. In the state courts it is often otherwise. That is, a plea bargain may be a trade of a guilty plea for a specific sentencing disposition, with which the state judge will normally concur. Of course, where, as is often the case in state courts, a defendant fails to make bail and remains in prison for a substantial amount of time pending trial, trial and sentencing become unnecessary altogether. At a certain point the defendant's guilty plea to reduced charges will mean a sentence for the time he has already served. In such situations it is at the original bail hearing that the sentencing decision is effectively made. Thus, since it is the prosecutor who decides whether or not to reach a plea bargain with each individual defendant, it is he who controls to a great extent the harshness of the sentence.

The federal system protects a defendant on trial in a criminal case fairly effectively from arbitrariness during the trial by providing for appeal in every criminal case.[26] However, jurors can and do exercise their virtually unfettered power, which is not subject to review, to protect defendants from what the jurors believe may be excessively harsh punishment under the law. The Court of Appeals for the Second Circuit recently reminded us that "the jury has 'power to bring in a verdict in the teeth of both law and facts.' "[27] Although jury acquittals in narcotics cases in our court are uncommon, mandatory minimum penalties of ten years or life in prison can only have the effect of making such acquittals more frequent. The disparate circumstances of each case and the varying quantities of narcotics involved make it clear that the jury will, more likely than not, consider such penalties too harsh in cases involving mitigating circumstances and small quantities of narcotics.

Under present federal law a person convicted of selling heroin or cocaine may be sentenced by the trial judge to a term of imprisonment of up to fifteen years.[28] In addition, a fine of up to $25,000 may be imposed. The sentence may be suspended. And the defendant sentenced to prison under the federal statute is eligible for parole after he has served one-third of his sentence, just as in the case of all other federal sentences.[29] If a prison term is imposed and not suspended, the judge must impose a parole term of not less than three years to follow any such term. In the case of any second or subsequent offense for which a prison term is imposed, the judge must impose a special parole term of not less than six years.[30]

On April 3, 1973, the Senate passed a bill which would require a judge to impose upon a second narcotics offender a mandatory minimum sentence of ten years.[31] He could impose more than ten years. The proposed maximum provided by the bill is thirty years. The mandatory minimum sentence of ten years must be imposed in addition to the sentence of up to fifteen years which may be imposed on second offenders. Such a double sentence is to be imposed on any defendant who had previously been convicted, on or after the effective date of the proposed new law, of illegally manufacturing, distributing, or dispensing one-tenth of an ounce of pure heroin or morphine or its equivalent and who, at the time he committed such violation, was not an addict. A person who has been so previously convicted is declared a "public menace." The statute further provides that if a person is found guilty of a third narcotics violation and has been previously convicted of selling one-tenth of an ounce of pure heroin or morphine and previously sentenced as a public menace, such defendant shall be sentenced, in addition to the sentence imposed of up to fifteen years, to life imprisonment. The imposition and execution of any such additional sentence may not be suspended and probation shall not be granted. However, any person sentenced to life imprisonment may be released on parole after serving not less than thirty years of his life sentence. Moreover, in no case shall any such additional term of imprisonment, including a life sentence imposed pursuant to these proposed provisions, run concurrently with any term of imprisonment imposed for such violation.

Prior to enactment of the present law[32] in October, 1970, providing for the sentencing of narcotics law violators, i.e., sellers and distributors, to a term of imprisonment of up to fifteen years, federal law provided for the imposition of mandatory minimum sentences in such cases—five years for the first offense and ten years for the second or any subsequent offense.[33] The harshness of the mandatory feature of those old provisions, together with the "no suspension–no parole" features, led judges and law-reform groups to seek more flexibility. In opposing the bill which was passed by the Senate on April 3, 1973, and which seeks to reinstitute mandatory minimum penalties for second and third offenders, Senator Ervin of North Carolina had this to say:

I am opposed to this amendment for two reasons. In the first place, I do not believe that the institution of mandatory minimum sentences will be effective in deterring these crimes or insuring proper punishment for the guilty. Experience shows and logic demonstrates that mandatory sentences in some cases actually encourage prosecutors to dismiss or break down charges to lesser offenses and encourage judges and juries to acquit the guilty. If a judge or jury believes the mandatory sentence does not fit the defendant under the circumstances, acquittal will be a great temptation.

The second objection I have to mandatory minimum sentences is the unfortunate restrictions they place upon the discretion of judges. Although, like other Americans, I do not always agree with the way in which judges exercise their traditional discretion in sentencing, I strongly believe in preserving this flexibility built into our system of criminal justice. It is the trial judge, not Congress, which hears all of the evidence, observes firsthand the particular defendant, and becomes acquainted with his background through the presentencing report. Mandatory sentences deprive trial judges of discretion to make the punishment fit the crime and the criminal.[34]

I believe that the sentencing of criminals is the most significant decision made by judges. As my colleague, the Honorable Judge Marvin E. Frankel, has so brilliantly discussed in his book *Criminal Sentences*,[35] there are virtually no standards to guide the judge's decision. In the federal system, there is presently no review of sentences. Yet the sentence decision has an effect which is more tangible and more significant to the defendant than any other decision in the criminal process. Being arrested may have varying consequences for a person.

Even being prosecuted may not in the end substantially change a person's life. But being sentenced to prison for a substantial period of time must have for the condemned a finality second only to death. The difference between receiving a suspended sentence with no prison term and going to prison for ten years is capable of conception only by the man who has been sentenced to such a term knowing that another person, similarly convicted, received two years or even a suspended sentence. Ten years is most often the maximum range of a sentence which a federal trial judge may impose. Narcotics cases are among the exceptions. And except for the maximum as defined by statute, the decision may be a more or less arbitrary one.

The presentence report[36] is supposed to aid the judge in determining what the sentence shall be; but apart from advising the judge of the defendant's prior criminal record, the report usually furnishes no other truly objective guides to sentencing. A defendant's background, family life, hobbies, employment record, and military record may be guides, but they are personal value judgments in the sentencing process. The weight to be given these vague attributes will vary from judge to judge. The seriousness of the crime committed is manifestly a major consideration in any sentence, but what may be serious to a judge in Kansas may not be equally serious to a judge in New York and vice versa. Likewise, even judges in the same court may disagree as to the seriousness of a particular offense.

In June, 1972, a Senate Committee on Criminal Law and Procedure was furnished a study of sentences in federal courts over the four-year period 1967–70 which showed considerable variation in length of sentences both within and between judicial districts. It also showed some interesting variations in length of sentences as between whites and blacks. In interstate theft cases, for example, 28 percent of white defendants received prison sentences as opposed to 48 percent for blacks. In postal theft cases it was 39 percent for whites as opposed to 48 percent for blacks.[37] For fiscal year 1970 the Federal Bureau of Prisons reported that the average length of sentences for white federal prisoners was 42.9 months as compared to 57.5 months for blacks.[38]

Last year the United States Attorney for the Southern District of New York made a study of sentences over a six-month period, May–October, 1972, in the Southern District court. Although he found no differentiation in sentencing in that court as between blacks and whites, he did find that only 36 percent of the white-collar criminals who were convicted went to jail as opposed to 53 percent of those convicted for nonviolent common crimes.[39]

There is another reason, as I have suggested, why the

sentencing function of judges is so significant. The fact is that few of those who are charged with crime actually go to trial. Indeed, only a small minority of defendants assert their constitutional right to a jury trial. The vast majority enter pleas of guilty. Consequently, the only substantial role a judge plays in a case where the defendant pleads guilty is at the time of sentencing.

Once a defendant is convicted and then sentenced by a judge, the defendant enters another stage of the criminal justice system: prison life. Here the criminal defendant is once again at the mercy of officials who exercise power and authority largely without rules.

The subjection of prisoners to arbitrary decisions of prison officials was well illustrated in the case of *Sostre v. Rockefeller*,[40] which was before me four years ago, and in the case of *Morales v. Schmidt*,[41] which was before Federal Judge Doyle of the Western District of Wisconsin in 1972. Sostre petitioned my court for release from solitary confinement, which he had endured for over a year. The evidence established that Sostre was treated in this way, "not because of any serious infraction of the rules of prison discipline, or even for any minor infraction, but because Sostre was being punished specially by the Warden" for his legal and political activities and beliefs.[42]

There was little difficulty in finding an ostensibly legitimate excuse for sending Sostre into solitary confinement. The warden could rely on such broad prison rules as the following: that an inmate obey orders "promptly and fully" and that inmates answer all questions put to them by prison officials "fully and truthfully." [43] The New York Correction Law at the time granted absolutely unfettered discretion[44] to wardens to commit prisoners to solitary confinement "until [they] shall [have been] reduced to submission." The statute was changed in 1970 without really affecting the scope of the warden's discretion. Now wardens "may keep any inmate confined . . . [separately] . . . for such period as may be necessary for maintenance of order or discipline." [45]

The decision to punish a prisoner in this way may be made by a prison warden without formal proceedings. The warden is only required to afford the prisoner a "reasonable opportunity to explain his actions." [46] And this is the case despite the fact that the placement of a prisoner in solitary confinement is often "dehumanizing in the sense that it is needlessly degrading." [47]

In *Morales*, Judge Doyle said:

> With respect to the intrinsic importance of the challenges [to the prison system], I am persuaded that the institution of prison probably must end. In many respects it is as intolerable within the United States as was the institution of slavery, equally brutalizing to all

involved, equally toxic to the social system, equally subversive of the brotherhood of man, even more costly by some standards, and probably less rational.[48]

Aside from the vagaries of prison life, prisoners are also subject to the totally unguided discretion of parole officials. In the parole system, we again find the exercise of authority without rules or standards to channel the decision-making function. At a First and Second Circuit Sentencing Institute in January, 1973, a member of the United States Board of Parole frankly admitted that he knew of no specific criteria by which the board made its determinations.

It is therefore easy to understand the description which the federal parole board has given of its operations in one of its official booklets:

Voting is done on an individual basis by each member, and the Board does not sit as a group for this purpose. Each member studies the prisoner's file and places his name on the official order form to signify whether he wishes to grant or deny parole. The reasoning and thought which led to his vote are not made a part of the order, and it is therefore impossible to state precisely why a particular prisoner was or was not granted parole.[49]

Of course, there is no way to explain disparities in results when there are no definable standards by which specific results are reached.

Some Views on Bringing Law and Order to the Sentencing Process

The preceding observations bring us to the second part of this analysis—some views on what might be done to bring more law and order to the sentencing process. It is said that criminal penalties are imposed by society for any one or more of five purposes:[50]

1. For retribution or revenge against the wrongdoer
2. For preventive detention—to restrain the wrongdoer during his confinement
3. For specific or individual deterrence—that is, to discourage the wrongdoer from committing crimes after his release
4. For general deterrence—to deter others from the same illegal conduct
5. To rehabilitate or reform the wrongdoer

Our present system of sentencing is concededly rather ineffective in accomplishing the last three purposes. The first two—retribution against and detention of a very small minority of wrongdoers—the system does seem to be accomplishing.

The reason that the sentencing system has such limited effectiveness in curbing crime seems to be that our society has not and will not commit the required resources to ameliorate the social conditions which breed criminal conduct and to "habilitate" or "rehabilitate" major law violators. Indeed, it does appear that no amount of money for improving social conditions will be effective as long as crime pays so well.

This is particularly true of the narcotics traffic. The convictions of narcotics agents and police officers for selling hard drugs tell us that no amount of money spent on better housing and better schools and better prisons will reduce the number of narcotics sellers as long as there are millions to be made in a society where it appears that only money counts. The problem of the illegal sale of narcotics is not to be solved by harsher and harsher penalties for pushers but by taking the profit out of selling narcotics. Our energies should therefore be devoted to finding ways to accomplish this end. If we find this solution, then one problem which has moved us frantically back to the severe mandatory minimum penalties concept will have vanished.

We will, nevertheless, be left with the realization that our society is not committed to a more rapid elimination of the crime-breeding syndrome or the remaking of a criminal. With this in mind, it seems to me that we should candidly face the fact that the only purposes that a sentence serves are retribution, preventive detention, and, in some cases, individual deterrences. If this is correct, if these are the only purposes, then the mandatory-sentence advocates have won a new adherent. However, my agreement with the mandatory-penalty school is very limited and is forced by the disheartening reality which I have cited.

First, I believe that mandatory penalties should be graduated, relatively short, and imposed only in conjunction with a system which grants every first offender a suspended sentence and an appropriate period of probation, with an exception for certain particularly heinous offenses, such as premeditated murder and consumer poisoning. In the case of monetary frauds, first offenders should, in addition, be required to make restitution. After the first offense, a short mandatory prison term of up to one year, legislatively defined for each crime, would be imposed. If there are exceptional or unusual mitigating circumstances, such as the imminent death of the defendant or his providing crucial testimony for the government, a suspended sentence may be recommended by the sentencing judge, whose written recommendation and reasons therefor must receive the approval of a reviewing panel. For the third offense, a much longer mandatory sentence of up to three years for each crime would be legislatively provided, with the same provisions for a suspended sentence. For the fourth offense, again, a longer mandatory sentence of five years would be provided, with the same provisions for suspended sentence. The fifth offender would be mandatorily sentenced to a term of five years. A similar mandatory sentence of five years would then be imposed for every offense thereafter.

For heinous crimes like murder, first offenders would receive a mandatory sentence which would vary according to the category of crime committed. Second offenders would receive very long mandatory sentences, depending on the crimes involved. Again, sentences could be suspended by the sentencing judge, but such suspensions would be subject to review.

This system contemplates that parole boards would continue to exist only for the release of prisoners for compelling humanitarian reasons. Prisoners judged mentally incompetent would of course be referred for treatment or would be confined in institutions if they cannot be treated and are dangerous to themselves or others.

Juveniles, youth offenders, and young adult offenders up to the age of twenty-six would continue to be treated the way they presently are treated in the federal system.[51] The judge would continue to have the power to treat young people as such, suspend their sentences up to the age of twenty-six, and commit them for study and treatment.[52]

The system also contemplates that all victimless crimes, such as alcoholism, drug use, and nonorganized prostitution, would be removed from the criminal justice system entirely and placed within a treatment system. It also contemplates that all gambling would be legalized.

In sum, we must take a fresh look at our criminal sentences to rationalize their purpose, to bring order to the system, and to eliminate meaningless disparities. The proposals which I have just made may be restated in a simplified manner like this:

1. No person should be sentenced to prison for a first offense, except for the most blameworthy offenses, such as premeditated murder.
2. Judges should have no discretion, except as indicated, in actually sentencing defendants to prison. The sentence should be specifically prescribed in each case by the legislature.
3. Suspended sentences should be strictly limited and subject to review.
4. The length of sentence should depend exclusively on the number of times a person has been convicted of a crime and on the seriousness of those crimes.

5. After the first offense, imprisonment should be for a short, definite term, perhaps six months on the average, and for a maximum of one year, depending on the seriousness of the crime, with increasingly longer sentences to be imposed after the second offense.
6. Victimless crimes would not be dealt with by the traditional criminal justice system.

Since punishment and individual deterrence are the purposes of the sentence, all other punishment, such as the imposition of lawless punishment on prisoners and the denial of employment to them after their release, should be eliminated.

The combination of these six considerations would create a sentencing regime in which less unguided discretion resided in the trial judge, in which the goal in dealing with youths and first offenders would be to reintegrate them into society rather than to punish or segregate them, in which imprisonment for longer than a year would be reserved for intractable offenders, and in which the stated purposes of imprisonment would be to punish the individual offender and to deter him from committing further crimes.

Such a system would have several salutary effects. Most importantly, it would eliminate the lawless discretion now exercised by judges. To say that a judge through the exercise of his or her presently uncharted discretion can in every case fashion punishment to fit not only the crime but the individual is to say that a judge is not only ordained by God but that he or she is God.

Second, it would eliminate gross disparities in sentencing. In nearly all categories of cases, federal judges as a group show little consistency in sentencing practices. The different treatment that similar offenders get has no objective basis in law, nor is it necessarily a reflection of any differences between the offenders or the crimes they have committed. The disparity in sentencing in cases such as draft evasion is purely and simply a function of the judges who impose the sentence. As Judge Frankel has put it, "Sentences [are] not so much in terms of defendants, but mainly in terms of the wide spectrums of character, bias, neurosis, and daily vagary encountered among occupants of the trial bench." [53]

Just like the parole boards, which I mentioned a few moments ago, federal judges are not required to articulate the underlying reasons for the sentences which they impose. Judges have neither adequate information nor sufficient time or training to make a meaningful disposition of every individual defendant's case. Even with more information and more specific sentencing standards, judges would act according to their own predilections in most cases, since the criteria would necessarily be vague, and a few factors among many relevant factors could always be cited to support a particular sentencing determination.

There is a more serious flaw in the present system of limitless discretion. Discretion is exercised usefully only when it is exercised to accomplish a particular purpose. In the case of sentencing, discretion is thought to be a salutary tool in the hands of judges because it enables them to decide the appropriate treatment for differing offenders. This would make sense if the prison system did anything more than isolate convicts and punish them. In fact, however, this is all that the prison system does; and, I would venture to say, this is about all that any prison system is ever likely to accomplish. Since punishment and detention are all that prisons can accomplish, there is no sense to allowing discretion in the sentencing process. If the purpose of sentencing discretion is to maximize the goal of individual deterrence, the present system is likewise inappropriate.

Punishment is an effective device for altering conduct only if it is applied fairly and as a direct sanction against the conduct which is sought to be punished. Under the present sentencing system, however, punishment is not dispensed fairly because judges mete out punishment according to their own subjective and undisciplined standards.

Nor is punishment always a direct sanction against

illegal conduct under the present sentencing system. Punishment is often imposed not so much for the specific offense which the defendant has committed but because of the defendant's social background, his failure to have a job, or his lack of education. Punishment imposed in this manner loses its force as a symbol of society's disapproval of the defendant's criminal conduct; instead, it tells the defendant that society disapproves of him, that his character is deficient. The defendant knows that the kind of treatment he receives from the criminal process is not primarily a function of the crime he has committed. It is more likely to be a reflection of the judge's estimate of him as a person.

It is fair to say that the individualized prison sentence is the first blow to a defendant's integrity and self-esteem in a process which, through the prison and parole regime, will deal him many more blows before his release. By punishing the defendant for what he is rather than for what he has done, some sentencers loosen what may already be a fragile tie between the defendant and society. By the end of a substantial prison term, the tie may be irrevocably broken.

The system I have proposed, unlike the present one, might even make sense to the offender, who might then gain respect for the rule of law. And it might, in the long run, reduce crime by reintegrating offenders into society rather than disintegrating them in our prisons. Any honest observer of the present sentencing process, the prison system, and crime statistics would have to agree that the time for a change of approach has come.

In his book *Criminal Sentences*,[54] Judge Frankel proposes a middle course between the mandatory-sentence concept which I have proposed and the present system. His tentative suggestion is to control the judge's discretion without eliminating it entirely. The control mechanisms would include a codification of sentencing factors which the judge would be required to weigh in determining the sentence to be imposed in each individual case. A "detailed chart or calculus" would be used, and the sentence would be subject to review by appellate courts.[55] Judge Frankel candidly notes, however, that similar efforts "have been made without notable success in the past." [56] The system as applied by judges might not in the end differ much from the present one. At the same time, it would create virtually insurmountable technical problems and uncertainties, since the calculus to be applied would be complex, subjective, and constantly under attack by various groups.

I would suggest that if we are to move in a new direction, a truly different approach should be tried. The proposals I have outlined seem to have the virtues of simplicity and easy applicability. They would also bring to the system a certainty of punishment for would-be offenders. The deterrent effect of certainty might also be salutary.

We know very little about how to deal with our crime problem, and the American public has made notably little effort to improve the situation by dealing with the realities of the problem. Perhaps, therefore, making the sentencing process fairer and limiting its claimed purposes are the necessary first steps in reform of the criminal justice system. They are the first of many steps that are needed. But they are the beginning of a "law and order" approach to the problems of lawlessness in the criminal justice system.

III

Philosophical Perspectives
on Justice

James K. Feibleman

1

I N MY WILLINGNESS TO ACCEPT the invitation to address you today on the topic of justice I am aware that there must have been a large measure of temerity, for I do not profess to have the final word about anything; I have only some studied guesses which I favor over others, chiefly, perhaps, because they are mine. What aggravates the situation is that it marks a departure from my proper business, which is to aid the inquiry into the true nature of things by discovering a whole way of looking at the world. Now, however, I find myself undertaking the employment of abstract theories in the analysis of practice. But I am aware that it is still true, as Plato said, that "philosophers are apt to appear ridiculous when they enter upon public business" [1] and, more particularly, "when they enter the courts of law as speakers," [2] although he did add that those who have trained as court orators since their youth are apt to be "always talking against time, hurried on by the clock," for there is always another party to the suit, and "the other party does not permit them to talk about anything they please, but stands over them exercising the law's compulsion by reading the brief, from which no deviation is allowed." [3]

The search for the meaning of justice must begin with a decision concerning the method to be employed. Rational understanding begins with definitions.[4] In my efforts at understanding, I propose a new approach to the idea of definition: definition by inference from assumptions, that is to say, from presuppositions. We must ask what the term "justice" has meant in some typical theoretical and practical contexts. I am aware of course that all definitions are limitations and so apt to prove inadequate. Actual material existence and abstract logical structures both have a way of escaping into a depth and extent of complexity which puts them beyond all meager formulations. But they do mark the first phase of a rationality on its way to full systematization by means of axioms, rules of inference, and the proofs of theorems. Such later fully systematized stages stand or fall by the earlier. They are therefore vulnerable, and the more so since they are the more easily altered.

Before a definition can be discovered and adopted, I propose to obtain it from a combination of the rational with the empirical, which is, by the way, the only acceptable empirical technique, since empiricism is incapable of standing alone as a finished product. In the case of justice, this means deriving the meaning of the term from its actual uses in legal theory and then testing that meaning twice: once for consistency with its necessary position in ethics, and once for completeness against the hard facts of the experiences encountered in lawmaking and law enforcement by legislators, judges, administrators, lawyers, and police.

What I hope to arrive at in this fashion is, of course, a universal meaning, which can then be checked back against another set of samples selected with the proper degree of randomness. Our access to facts for this purpose is strictly limited. When men speak of looking at a topic universally, what they mean is looking at it earthwide and for the period of known history, which includes, unfortunately, only the last ten thousand years —a provincial view but at least one not limited to a specific date and place. The day is rapidly approaching when that will not do at all; but it will have to serve for the present.

If the definition of justice does not rise above the level of a captive concept in the hands of a single government—as when, for instance, men judge of what is just according to the American practice—then it can contribute little to legal theory. We want to be able to judge our own institutions as well as others, and for praise or blame; and this we cannot do without a conception which rises above them in some way. Those who charge that cultural relativism reduces all conceptions to functions of the society in which they were framed overlook the fact that their criticism is as culture-bound as the theory they are criticizing.

That there is a universal truth which transcends the laws of nations can be demonstrated to a secular and empirically minded age through the common understanding of the demand for justice and the ancillary need for a universal comprehension of the term. We must have absolute principles, not for the erroneous purpose of making absolute applications but in order to know what we are modifying when we encounter extenuating circumstances.

In all of the thousands of years that such a question has been seriously considered there has been no agreement about the meaning of justice, no accepted definition. But I take it this does not mean that there has been no common understanding. Only its formulation is wanting, a lack which has serious shortcomings but also some advantages in allowing to the administration of justice the requisite flexibility. There need be no inconsistency between an inflexible definition and a flexible administration provided the true nature of definition be understood. Things can be properly related only when they have first been properly distinguished. Rationality is not aided by a muddy empiricism in which principles and practices are hopelessly confused. Principles first must be learned from practice but then firmly separated and properly interrelated as principles before being returned to practice with a greatly increased power over it.

Let me put this in another way. An interest in the law for practical reasons is the business of the practicing lawyer. It is not the same, and it does not have the same results, as an interest in the law for theoretical reasons. Lawmakers no doubt must have both interests; but they rely as much on the previous work of the theorists as they do on their knowledge of the practices to which the laws they enact will be applied. Behind every charter of government, written or unwritten, there stands a philosophy, overt or covert.

In search of the theory of justice, I plan to look first (II) at some of the empirical evidence which is to be found in the administration of justice and next (III) at the same kind of evidence, but derived from injustice. Then (IV) I shall propose my own definition of justice and try to support it (V) by theoretical evidence from studies of ethics and morality as these have related to the state.

II

We need to glance first, then, at some examples of what the administration of justice as practiced seems to indicate concerning the meaning of justice. These examples, we will discover, offer empirical evidence for a particular kind of definition.

To begin with, it can be pointed out that laws are neither made in a vacuum nor administered in one. According to some, justice is binding on magistrates as well as on offenders, and so the concept needs to be defined in order to set goals for lawmakers and law-enforcers as much as for lawbreakers. Again, when a particular theory of justice has been adopted, this does not mean that practice will always conform to it. Too often men depart from that behavior which they know to be most conformable to the set of values to which they subscribe. This happens, for instance, when an action taken by an officer of a state differs from the morality which governs its citizens—and does so with their implicit or even express approval.

It is evident from an examination of the laws in effect in any Western nation that they are intended to cover every possible contingency and to do so in a perfectly consistent fashion. Whether they ever did so is another question. In private business as well as in public order, in the civil as well as the criminal law, care has been exercised over the years by those in authority to see that no situation can arise in which the legal requirements are not spelled out and the penalties not prescribed for any infractions. The requirement of consistency was met when the rules governing the duties of common carriers were applied to the railroads *in the same way* as they had been to the stagecoaches. The requirement of completeness was met when there were no longer any common carriers to which the governing rules did not apply.

Constitutions are written by men with the aim of total provision in mind; but lawmakers sit as a body and make themselves continuously available so that, as the society develops and unforeseen eventualities arise, new statutes can be enacted to provide for them. It was for this reason, for example, that the Sherman Antitrust Act and later all of the laws governing civil aeronautics were considered necessary. In short, there is always a determined effort to make the laws complete with respect to the activities of a given society, although the requirement of completeness for the laws has never been codified.

Another version of this requirement shows up in quite a different way. In actual law practice there is always present the appeal to an abstract principle of justice, and its applications are engineered through a series of adjustments which are continually being made. An unacknowledged but effective legal version of the principle which has come to be known as Occam's Razor calls for there to be no more laws than are necessary. People are unhappy with superfluous laws, which make them feel restricted in a way which is not beneficial to them or to the society; but there is a counterbalancing, equally unacknowledged, but also effective principle announced by Kant, which I have named Kant's Shaving Bowl, the legal version of which requires that there be as many laws as are necessary.[5] But without laws to regulate the new situations, there would be more unhappiness.

Laws and lawmaking machinery arise in the simple response to needs. Witness the federal regulative agencies which have sprung up in the last couple of decades: the Civil Aeronautics Authority and the Atomic Energy Commission, for instance. The laws tend to expand to cover whatever activities emerge which are potentially, at least, threats to the common good. Hence the Sherman Antitrust Act. There are laws now, for example, governing the securities business, the insurance companies, and labor relations, which had formerly been relatively free of regulation. The adjustments which are found necessary in order to keep the legal system a workable affair include those designed to preserve or restore consistency and those intended to keep pace with the requirement of completeness.

Justice may occur in practice simply as a response to the demand for order. This can even happen by chance, as it were. In England, the East India Company, which was chartered by Queen Elizabeth in 1600 to trade in what is now Indonesia, and which returned its first revenues from Sumatra by looting a Spanish galleon, ended by founding an empire; and by 1858, when Disraeli relieved the Company of its responsibilities and gave India to Queen Victoria, the English legal system had become so entrenched and so valuable that India, even after it had obtained its independence from England, retained the English system of law and law practices.[6]

The demand for order may make itself felt where a legal system already exists. Confusion results when laws are enacted which are more complex than the citizens can comprehend. No one in the United States is free from taxation, but few can understand the tax statutes. Too complex a structure is not an order but in the end amounts to a new and contrived kind of disorder. The enormous proliferation of laws in the United States at both the federal and state levels amounts itself to a kind of confusion. Laws which remain on the books after they have ceased to be enforced can always be revived and sometimes are, with the result that in many instances the citizens do not know exactly where they stand with respect to the law.

Government bureaucrats tend to forget that all of the revenues of the state eventually derive from the productivity of agriculture and manufacturing in much the same way that businessmen and farmers tend to forget that all of the property rights they enjoy and the enforcement of contracts upon which their profits depend rely entirely upon the stability of the state in which they hold citizenship. The enormous intricacy of the modern scientific-industrial nation often temporarily blinds men to the true state of affairs. Justice reaches upward at this point to insist that the legal order be a system. In human affairs, since injustice does occur, this works out to the demand for the restoration of that order to which the administration is already devoted.

But it may lead also to the demand for an essentially new order. The legal system thus far has been in every case a limited order. If a universal social order does exist—and there is every reason to hope that it may—

it has not yet been discovered. There are at the present time insuperable obstacles in the way. There has never been any question of concrete universals, since they will not be proved to exist until it is possible to ransack the universe; the question is only whether or not they are known, for they could exist and yet not be known. If justice be a universal, then we can say that universal standards of justice may exist but cannot be verified with certainty. The assumption of their existence, however, provides a background for less general instances of justice.

The point made by Charles S. Peirce, the classic American philosopher, about the necessary vagueness of generality[7] is supported in many common-law interpretations and indeed in the promulgation of most legislation. What is the "due process of law" referred to in the Fifth and Fourteenth amendments to the Constitution of the United States? There is certainly evidence of its vagueness in some of the judicial decisions which have issued from it.[8] There is a kind of principle of indeterminacy at work here which is akin to the principle of the same name in atomic physics: in a given legal procedure, such as in statutory interpretations, one part of a statute can be rendered precise only by allowing other parts to remain uncertain. The legislature, for example, can formulate a law with accuracy but then leave open the question of just how far its effectiveness extends; or it can state a law in general terms but then leave open the nature of its application.

Such a demand for order, however, must be distinguished from any particular order; for if too rigidly administered under rapidly changing circumstances, one particular order could function as a disorder. Back of such a situation there is an assumed requirement of justice, which can be as much abrogated by a narrow order as by a wide disorder. If it develops that laws need to be enlarged and extended, restricted or eliminated, or indeed modified in any way which a developing society may make necessary in order to eliminate inconsistencies which may have arisen in the body of laws under the wear and tear of practice, this does point to a hidden constant, an ideal parameter behind the limited formulations of the legal code.

That so many legal codes are provided with built-in self-corrective techniques is evidence for the existence of the law as an open system. An open system in the legal sense is one which is left free to exchange conditions with the rest of the society in which it exists to provide order; free, that is to say, to modify and be modified by material conditions. The laws of a society exist as its effort at self-regulation, and so they in turn are regulated by the society as it develops and changes. For no society is fixed forever; it is always under the necessity to interact with the human and nonhuman elements of its environment.

The lawmakers in a state endeavor to frame the laws in a perfectly coherent manner and one which covers every contingency. That a system of order is what is being interpreted in the administration of justice is shown by the three principles contained in Dicey's famous definition of the rule of law.[9] The supremacy of the law, the equality of all before the law, and their rights as defined and enforced by the courts make of the legal system a single inclusive and irrefrangible body of doctrine and procedure. This works out in practice to a facilitative rather than a restrictive, a regulative rather than a punitive, over-all effect. It aims to promote the welfare of individuals in such a way that they do not interfere with one another.

In laying down guidelines for what can and cannot be done, there is a consistency sought which suggests the grounds for a general assumption of justice. That laws are also brought into operation when they are not violated indicates a certain allowable behavior from which all conflict is eliminated. Since conflict may be defined as the material analogue of the logic of contradiction, a certain consistency is implied; and since the aim is to specify violations for all laws and to stipulate penalties for all violations, a certain completeness is implied also.

III

From considering justice, we now turn to injustice. What is it that the phenomenon of injustice may be said to indicate with respect to the meaning of justice? Injustice is a variety of disorder; it may be defined as disorder in society. Disorder is, loosely, the absence of order, but a more precise definition may be useful here. Cairns has in fact defined jurisprudence as "the study of human behavior as a function of disorder." [10] Elsewhere I have defined disorder as the extent to which the elements of a given order are distributed outside that order among the elements of other orders. [11]

I propose to argue here that as a matter of practical exigency injustice always has been a function of justice, requiring of necessity the administration and enforcement of the laws. The Corpus Juris Civilis promulgated by the Roman emperor Justinian about A.D. 535 conceived of law in terms of remedies, not as a matter of rights and duties but of liabilities to certain actions. Injustice could occur only within the confines of the acceptance of a legal system.

I am speaking of justice here, of course, in the limited sense in which it describes adherence to a particular order. Injustice in the universal sense of the term is another matter and would have to have a wider meaning. The very existence within a social order of an established set of procedures and a trained set of men to administer them is evidence enough that with the establishment of a system of laws goes the assumption that some of the laws will be disobeyed on some occasions. The recognition of an offense, whether a crime, a misdemeanor, or a tort, negatively affirms the existence of law; and the number of statutes intended to cover all offenses affirms that it is the nature of the law to be complete.

With regard to a society in the round, the demand for a system of order makes itself felt most strongly in revolutionary situations. The systems of legal order presently prevailing in France and the Soviet Union were born of violent revolutions. Anarchy cannot serve as the basis for the stability of a society. One important consequence of this is that, while every revolution takes place to bring to an end a particular system of order, it is always followed by the establishment of another system of order and often by one which is even more intolerable than the one it replaced. If justice is a system of order, injustice is disorder; but while injustice on a small scale can be purely random, in terms of our definition of disorder injustice on a large scale, as the organizations of pirates and brigands in the Mediterranean and the Caribbean in the late nineteenth century graphically illustrate, can be a system, too; and yet we shall have to say that injustice is the property of a lesser system of order, one less inclusive than that which is provided by justice.

That there will always be a need for the administration of law depends upon a number of factors. In the first place, law is not always punitive; it is also regulative and facilitative, so that if no laws were ever broken there would still be a need for administration. But there is little danger of that; for, in the second place, no matter how law-abiding a society may be, there is always a minority of lawbreakers. Anyone may infract a law through thoughtlessness, carelessness, or ignorance, but in a more deliberate way there is always a very considerable percentage of willful lawbreakers and of pathological cases; habitual criminals will never cease to exist.

Even more dangerous situations will continue to occur. As we have just seen, injustice as well as justice may be organized and indeed often is. Most criminals who have acted in any consequential way have persuaded themselves and sought to persuade others that, to the contrary, it was they who were moving against injustice and that in so doing they were preserving a system of justice. Robin Hood was neither the first nor the last man to claim that in robbing the rich to give to the poor he was righting a wrong; and Al Capone could insist that, by breaking the prohibition against alcohol, he was helping to satisfy a legitimate need. Injustice, as a matter of fact, tends to keep pace with justice. The awesome power of organized crime in the United States today illustrates clearly that, as a society becomes complex, it often is matched in its complexity by criminal systems of subversion.

There are other factors which must be taken with extreme seriousness. The first of these is that men by nature have ambivalent drives, only one set of which is peaceful and constructive. The evidence of prehistory, which has been greatly expanded in recent decades through discoveries of fossil man and his artifacts, shows that we have inherited from our remotest ancestors, the hominids, a deep physiological as well as psychological aggression, which I here define as the alteration of the material environment, both organic and inorganic, for the purposes of somatic need-reduction. This has been the inevitable result of hundreds of thousands and even millions of years of hunting culture, which included cannibalism, and of nomadic existence, in which men had to kill to live. In a mere ten thousand years of settled civilization we have not lost the habit, to which our slaughterhouses and wars offer mute but vivid evidence. The need for destruction at this stage in the history of the human species probably lies deep in the genes.

The somatic need to continue existence is carried out, then, by an aggression that takes two forms: destructive and constructive, both of which are necessary. In order to exist together, men have had to organize their societies into states, and it has become the business of the state to limit the destructive form of aggression internally by means of laws. In this way the state has grown into a community of law, and a well-ordered state into one possessing a system of law. Externally it has become the business of the state to expand the destructive form of aggression. There are not many states, if indeed there are any, which can claim no injustice in foreign relations. Lawlessness at this level is all but officially acknowledged.[12]

Added to this picture is an even more distressing fact, and that is the frequent success of injustice. Plato was a great dramatist of the truth, and so he allowed his adversaries to present eloquent arguments in their dialectical debates with Socrates. In *Republic* I[13] and in the *Gorgias*[14] both Thrasymachus and Callicles expatiate at length on the rewards of injustice. Granted that they dealt only in half-truths; but I remind my hearers that half-truths, though half false, are also half true. It is bound to be a temptation to financially successful wrong-doers to remember that virtue is not always rewarded and vice not always punished. Too many of our captains of industry have stolen and butchered their way to fortunes only to die peacefully at the end of long lives in their hospital trundle beds. The attractiveness of law and order and justice will have to rest on other grounds if it is to succeed at all.

That injustice does succeed in large measure is evidence that there may be other grounds for it, although this tends to have more weight at some periods of history than at others. In periods of relative social stability, feelings of personal obligation and fears of sanction cooperate to insure compliance with the law; but in such periods, when the stability of the social fabric is threatened from without as well as from within, the fear of social chaos operates with increased force. All responsible citizens are aware of the consequences of the breakdown of order and—what is the same thing—of law.

Short of the paroled mental patient, with a homicidal intent and a gun, and like situations, which would call out the instinct of self-preservation, with its resultant violence, in even the most peaceful and law-abiding of citizens, coercive law enforcement need only be held in the background to serve as a deterrent to the average citizen. But there is always the criminal who by his behavior insists on its exercise. Given the makeup of a large population, the ideal of perfection contained in the theory of justice and its rule of law can never be absolutely attained in practice.

However, what is true of individual man in little—that he is by nature a fighting animal—extends to his society in large. States are permitted to do what individuals are not permitted to do unless acting for the state. This has confused many a simple-minded citizen who has at different times in his life been called upon to act in different capacities. What the state would punish him for doing in private life—murder, for instance—it is prepared to punish him for *not* doing when he finds himself a soldier and in battle.

The violence of a society, I regret to report, is a function of its total energy. This may make it a necessary precondition for relative calm within a society that its aggressive drives be allowed full scope beyond its borders. Societies famous for being "law-abiding" in their day, as England was in the nineteenth century, may have been so because the aggressive drives of the citizens were allowed and even officially encouraged abroad. A *Pax Britannica* was established throughout the world by means of wars of conquest conducted on four continents, but this may have been what made possible so much adherence to law and order at home, just as, several millennia earlier, the widespread "Roman peace" was based on the readiness of the Roman legions to fight. Similarly, in the United States, in the same period, the western frontier was the scene of the exercise of violence, as our artists and writers as well as our historians have been at pains to tell us. It may be that the defeats incurred in two small but very expensive Asian wars have turned us in upon ourselves, with results in a degree of domestic lawlessness and random aggression that is becoming somewhat unbearable.

Man alone among the animals is capable of doing things wrong because he alone has a choice. It is because of the existence of disorder that the administration of order is needed. There are few people who have not at some time or other broken the laws; but all laws are not equally important except *as* laws, and few offenders have ever voluntarily submitted to punishment or correction for the infraction of laws which even they considered just. The probability of the occurrence of injustice is therefore very high, and so justice must be founded on the use or the threat of force. The general assumption that an abstract justice has concrete demands is the reason why the laws, for all their supremacy within the state, must still face the requirements of equity. Justice may come into conflict with other goods, for it sometimes happens that goods conflict. We speak of just and unjust laws, which would seem to indicate that justice is higher than law. Central to justice is the respect for the individual as both rational and responsible, and the law distributes its sanctions accordingly.

There is an appeal to the meaning of justice as defined by the actions of men when they defy a court injunction on the plea that the law they are disobeying is not a valid law. Presumably they mean that under a higher notion of justice the law itself is unjust. This has occasionally been the case with the leaders of labor unions, who rely upon the numerical strength of their supporters as measured by union membership to uphold them against the authority of the courts. Justice implies the rule of law not only over men but also over laws. There is a suggestion here, too, of the laws as forming a system in which some particular law does not consistently belong.

How is a government to keep the activities of its various branches consistent when it is compelled to delegate its powers as a matter of practical necessity? Thus in 1971 we had the spectacle of a surgeon general doing everything possible to discourage the sale and use of tobacco and, at the same time, a Department of Agriculture subsidizing tobacco farmers. That inconsistencies in bodies of laws do arise may be due in part to the proliferation of federal agencies whose operation is semi-independent, without anyone being responsible for their coordination. There are inconsistencies, too, in the order of importance of law-enforcement procedures. Issuing tickets for parking in no-parking zones often takes up more of the policemen's hours than pursuing heroin pushers, rapists, or murderers.

A final argument for the existence of injustice as part

of the demand for a system of order is to be found in the position of the criminal. He has no conception at all of his dependence upon the stability of the social order he infracts. If the system were to break down altogether, the money he steals would be worthless and the influence he buys would be without the power to shield him. The value to him of his disobedience is a function of the obedience of most others. Everyone cannot afford to be a criminal; the system will not support it. On the other hand, everyone can be honest and obey the law, and this the system will support. I am reminded of the open letter a grateful reader once wrote to Dale Carnegie, author of *How to Win Friends and Influence People.* The reader said that he had found the book useful, but he hoped that not everyone would buy it and follow its advice because, obviously, this would cancel his advantage.

IV

Having, I hope, found some evidence for a definition of justice both in the actual administration of justice and in the gross facts of injustice, I turn next to a statement of my definition of justice; but first we must understand it in its most general sense. Justice as such is the demand for order: everything in its proper place or relation. It is the material analogue of the logical principle of identity.[15] In a certain sense, then, the demand for order is a demand for unity, the proper fitting of parts in the whole.[16] But order quite simply means a one-to-one correspondence with the positive integers, and so it must be evident that what I am talking about here is no simple order. Justice would of course be impossible without social order, and the maintenance of social order rests upon social laws. Now a law is an established regulation which applies equally throughout a society and is backed by force.[17] Thanks to the existence of law-enforcement machinery, the state intervenes directly when laws are broken (criminal law) or stands ready to intervene indirectly when appealed to (civil law). It is the laws which organize society and so make of society a state, though statehood rests not just on a collection of laws but on a system of laws.[18] Justice, then, will be concerned with a system of laws.[19]

It is obvious that here we need a definition of "system." A system in the broad sense may be regarded as a set of elements having a common property—in the narrow sense, it may be regarded as a set of sentences in which every sentence is either an axiom or a theorem, in which case there are the further requirements of consistency, completeness, and categoricity. I shall be talking here chiefly about systems in the broad sense; but when I refer to the system of laws which justice demands, I shall find it necessary to raise the questions of consistency, completeness, and categoricity.

A legal system is consistent if none of the laws conflict. A legal system is complete if all of the laws in the system can be shown to be laws of the system and if all of the laws which could be laws of the system can be shown to be laws in the system. In other words, consistency requires that all of the laws in the system belong in the system, and completeness requires that all of the laws that belong in the system are in the system.[20]

Categoricity is more difficult to explain. Perhaps it should first be pointed out that when the concepts of logic and mathematics are applied to concrete systems, it is always with appropriate modifications and interpretations. With this provision in mind, a "category" may be defined as a class of sets with similar structure.[21] Categoricity uniquely determines the system it describes. If any two interpretations satisfying the axioms are isomorphic, then the system can be said to be categorical. That the laws of a society are categorical is guaranteed by the fact that they all follow from the same theory of reality and all exist on the same level of analysis.

Understanding the terms "justice," "law," and

"system," then, in the senses defined above, I am ready with my definition: *Justice is the demand for a system of laws.*

Now a system of laws, like any system, must be made up of axioms and the theorems (in this case, the laws) which follow from them. But which axioms? Obviously, in a given society, those which are constructions of the values whose preeminent reality the members of the society accept in their beliefs, embody in their artifacts, and aim at in their actions. Without a single consistent and comprehensive set of values, accepted by the members in feeling if not in principle, no society would be viable. The aim of a system of laws is to achieve in practice those values which the axioms represent.

Justice under the law proves to depend upon what theory of justice the laws embody. Thus Aristotle's criterion that "the just is the proportional" [22] would yet depend upon what it is that the society values most, upon what it is that is being proportioned.

When a state establishes a system of laws, it does not do so arbitrarily or by canvassing the wishes of individual citizens but always by looking to the embodiment of the ideal of justice, however vague such a conception may seem to be as it hovers in the background of more specific stipulations. The different legal systems found in different states are partly the results of human choice; for man alone, it seems, has this option before him. But because much of what he does in a sociocultural way is laid out for him by the exigencies of material conditions as these exist in a given date and place, his options are limited and his actions are partly, at least, the result of necessity.

What we are dealing with in any society, then, is not mere laws but a system of laws, since a social order is a system. More specifically, justice is employed to guard against the assumption, often made in practice, that disorder can prevail. Logically, if justice is the material analogue of the principle of identity, injustice appeals to the truth of the unexcluded middle. In social affairs, justice would call for the making of laws and injustice for their administration. Thus justice is tied to the defense of social order and therefore to the restoration of order through the rejection of disorder or injustice.

I have been talking in ideal terms. Any actual legal system will tend to be a partially ordered system, and a partially ordered system is one which meets to some extent the requirement of consistency but not the requirement of completeness.[23] That is to say, not all of the laws in the system belong in the system, and not all of the laws that belong in the system are in the system. Contradictions and incompletenesses occur, but not in sufficient numbers to cancel altogether the effectiveness of the system so far as the social order is concerned.

The definitions of justice which I have given in

earlier works occurred in connection with ethics and politics and are congruent with partial ordering. In my ethics I have defined justice as the restoration of good,[24] and in my politics I have defined it as conformity to the good.[25] The good is the name for a qualitative bond, and this is the typical kind of piecemeal affair which calls for a description in terms of partial ordering; but the good is also a combining force, a unifying property, as Plato suggested when he placed it at the apex of his hierarchy of ideas.[26] But here I am looking to the broader meaning implied in both definitions.

In any social system there are too many variables to be calculated correctly by any of the means presently at our disposal. The demand for the *ideal* of justice is a demand for a well-ordered system, a perfect legal system, which would be both consistent and complete. The *actuality* of justice is a partially ordered legal system. The *direction* of justice is the movement from the actual to the ideal, present in the aims of those who would seek improvement in the legal system.

We might speak then of *ideal* justice as the ideal of law and of *actual* justice as the actual system of laws, one which includes statutes, unwritten laws, courts, judges, and lawyers, as well as administrative and enforcement officers; and finally we might speak of *directional* justice as the lawmaking machinery consisting of legislators and their authorization. I have talked about ideal justice as natural justice. Directional justice is what is aimed at by enactment. It is aimed at equally in the framing of constitutional law and statute law. It is intended to promote public utility, in Hume's sense.

But it is at this level of actual justice that my definition will be challenged, and so it will be well to say a few words in extension and explanation. An established system of laws is one which is in effect in an actual society and remains in force, though perhaps changed from time to time, until overthrown. It exists within the individuals who are the members of the society; it exists within the society as its established institutions, regulating the individuals, their interest groups, their actions, and their artifacts (or property); and it exists also in the external relations of the society. Let us consider each of these briefly.

First, as to its existence within individuals. To say that an established legal order exists within the individuals in a society means that covertly it is the way in which they would wish to be governed. They have beliefs of a fundamental nature, of the majority of which they are not conscious. This becomes most evident when they are called on for precipitate action, which is usually from beliefs not deliberately held. There are of course levels of belief, some lying much more deep than others and hence harder to recall. Such are, for instance, the more fundamental beliefs concerning the nature of reality which the individual holds in common with his fellows in the society, beliefs which of course would differ from society to society. There are other beliefs which exist at the same profound level and which are private; but these are rare, and we shall not have to deal with them here. Meanwhile, it is this consistency of the part within the whole that gives to the individual who obeys the law what Mill called "the sentiment of justice," the feeling of what is right.

Next, as to the established system of laws within the society. For a legal system to be consistent, it must be applicable; and for it to be complete, it must be compatible with the fundamental convictions of a majority of the citizens. To say that an established legal order exists among them means that overtly they have consented to be governed in this fashion. Such public beliefs are embodied in institutions, first and foremost in the institution of the state, with its administration of law.

Finally, we must consider the extension of the established system of laws outside the state. Justice requires that the social order be the largest possible under the circumstances. A lesser order, as we shall note later, can function as a disorder in international society. The system of laws established within a single society cannot be too much in conflict with those of other states without damage to justice.

Against my definition it will probably be argued that it is too broad, that under it a tyranny is a social order and so meets the demand for order. National Socialism —the order established by Hitler and the Nazis—would seem to satisfy my definition, it will be claimed, for it did meet the demand for a system of laws. To this criticism I can offer two denials.

Tyranny, however systematic, does not meet two of the requirements of order, the one within the individual citizens and the other outside the state, for the following reasons.

A state with an established tyranny, in which the tyrant rules by promulgation, is still an orderly government, however undesirable it may be from some points of view, since it satisfies the requirement of consistency which is set by the definition of justice. It satisfies this requirement, however, only at the expense of completeness. Order in the sense in which I use the term includes order in the individual citizens as well as between them. Order, as Plato said in the *Republic*, is order within the soul as well as within the state. Toynbee drives a distinction between a dominant minority which rules by charm and has the approval of those who are ruled, and a dominant minority which rules by force and so operates despite the disapproval of most citizens.[27] The former condition meets the requirements of my definition better than the latter.

It is possible, of course, for an absolute monarchy to have the approval of a majority of the citizens, as when, for instance, the monarch is believed to be divinely appointed and no other form of government is known. This was probably the case in ancient Egypt, when, for many millennia, no one seems to have questioned the right of the rulers to rule. So much for conformity within the state, which is never perfect. With regard to the extension of the established system of laws outside the state, the prevalence of wars throughout the ten thousand years of known history would seem to indicate that the requirement of completeness is never altogether met and seldom met at all. The situation in this regard grows worse rather than better, for in terms of transportation and communication the world is a much smaller place than it was; and the requirement of completeness imposed by the definition of justice as the demand for a system of laws extending outside the state lacks the needed conformity if many states are to exist together. Put otherwise, in a projected global state, the demand for completeness would turn into a demand for consistency.

Any political order can be disturbed as much from within as from without. The preservation of order requires an equilibrium to be maintained without any disturbance that could challenge it as an order. Thus one principle of order is that it must be wider than any contained disorder. There are serious and even crucial issues in which practical exigencies take precedence over moral considerations. When the crime rate is low, it is possible to concentrate on the criminal and on whether justice is being done him, and to complain, as Taft did when he was Chief Justice of the Supreme Court, that our criminal law is a disgrace. But when the crime rate reaches the proportions it has assumed today, then attention shifts to the protection of society. An order can be imposed by conflict but can be maintained only by consent. But an order may deliberately make provisions for the inclusion of lesser conflict, as is the case, for instance, when business competition exists within an economic order.

V

Let us see, finally, how an ideal of justice, which exists within individuals as their beliefs, within the society as its institutions, and beyond the society as its relations with other societies, can be viewed when interpreted in terms of ethics.[28]

Human societies are not mere collections of men; they are organizations of men and materials, the addition to men of raw materials and artifacts: mere territories as well as formed materials which have been altered through human agency for human uses. Cultures are the most complex material organizations known, for they include human individuals with their brains and nervous systems; but they include also artifacts, interpersonal relations, and brain-artifact relations. They differ from time to time and from place to place, and their contents differ: different sorts of artifacts and different sorts of people, who, even though all belonging to the same species, lead different sorts of lives because of two variable factors: the peculiarities of the environment and the idiosyncrasies of explicit ideals; and finally, as we should expect, there are different sorts of organizations and, with them, different sorts of laws and law practices. The key to what holds all these disparate parts together may be looked for in morality. A morality is the kind of behavior which is called for in a given environment in terms of a given set of stated ideals of the good. It is what happens to a given theory of ethics when confronted by an inescapable set of material conditions. A morality is a set of values by means of which the members of a society live together. When that society becomes a state, its morality is established by codification: laws are codified morality. The established laws and law practices endeavor not only to particularize the accepted morality but also to enforce and defend it.

Individuals within a society retain two sets of schemes of belief, two sets of retention schemata, which we can now recognize as moral: one set which they share with their fellow citizens and another set which they hold alone. The scheme which they share with their fellows is the public sector; it reflects the morality and guides the individual toward conventional behavior and the observance of laws. The private sector of the retention schemata may be aberrant or it may not. Since all activities are conducted in terms of beliefs, the private beliefs may lead to aberrant behavior and to infractions of the laws. Not all such infractions are so rational, however; there are also infractions on impulse or from psychotic motives.

Conscience is the awareness on the part of an individual of an obligation to obey his beliefs. When these issue from the public retention schema, they impel the individual toward obedience to the laws of his society; but occasionally the beliefs contained in the private retention schema cut across that impulse and thwart it. When Lieutenant (jg.) D. L. Mendenhall, the bombardier-navigator of an F-4 Phantom, reported that "Whatever our feelings about the war, we're still dropping our bombs—and we enjoy it," [29] he was admitting that his own misgivings with respect to the public morality were too slight to interfere with his actions. But when a man asks himself whether with a clear conscience he can obey a law that he considers unjust, he is appealing not to his conscience as such but to its contents, which may contain a different morality. When Oskar Schindler saved hundreds of German Jews from the Auschwitz extermination camp through deliberate misrepresentations to the Nazi authorities, he was hearing a different drummer.[30]

Such moral difficulties occur within the individual more often when the society is changing, for change usually occurs in one institution before influencing the whole society, as in a new religious insight or a new political ideal, and individuals tend to be institutionally oriented.

Now allow me to recapitulate. Justice, you will remember, is the demand for a particular kind of order— for a system of order. And order is implemented in a system of laws. The laws themselves establish a particular morality. The morality follows from a theory of ethics and is enforced by the state. Morality is the essence of society, and every society has a morality; but the moralities differ from society to society as the societies themselves differ. The morality of a society is the only kind of order which is suitable to that society and is therefore the only kind which can satisfy justice.

When the society changes, the morality changes with it. The administration of law is the carrying-out of the kind of justice a particular morality requires.

According to my theory, then, the forging of the laws of a state, together with their administration and revisions, is the outcome of the encounter and resolution of two opposed forces: the morality, which is handed down from the deep-set convictions of the members of the society, and the peculiar material requirements, which are a product of the brute encounters of sense experience. The resultant legal system derives its consistency from the morality and its completeness from the experiences. It might be added parenthetically that the morality itself issues from a theory of reality, or ontology, which, however implicit and unrecognized, nevertheless stands behind it.

And just as ethics is anchored securely somewhere between the theories of ontology and the practical exigencies of concrete moralities, so laws are anchored somewhere between abstract morality and practical exigency; both change, and therefore so must the laws. It must be recalled, however, that laws are not mere collections—they are systems; and though operated by short-lived individuals, they are legal systems within such long-lasting institutions as the state. The necessary continuity is preserved, but that is why the laws do not direct society but only regulate it. But they regulate it in a particular direction, more specifically, in that direction which was the one selected when the laws were chosen in the first place. The laws implement a particular morality; but because they are laws and because they are established, changes in the laws are apt to lag behind changes in the morality. For the laws were chosen after the morality, and thenceforth they follow it at a safe distance. The laws forbidding abortion in the United States will have to be changed to conform to the morality permitting abortion if respect for the law itself is not to be injured.

That the laws follow the shifts in morality, even though at a discreet distance, is most evident perhaps in the changes which take place in the decisions of the Supreme Court of the United States. If the Court does not exactly follow election returns, as has been claimed, it does follow public opinion in its alternations of conservatism and evolution; and public opinion is a good index to the implicit and prevailing morality. The liberal policy of the Warren Court of the 1960s makes an interesting contrast with the Taft Court of the 1920s.[31] Morality is dictated by the ideals of the leading institution, and business, in that interim period between the two Courts named, had been downgraded.

The police, the district attorneys, and the local courts enforce some laws and allow others to remain unenforced. The decision to enforce or not is made on

the basis of shifts which are left in the background
morality. No one can name or describe the background
morality, but its influence is felt no less strongly for
that. Thus it may happen that those who are responsible
for changes in the morality may run counter to the
laws. Sometimes they make revolutions, though not all
revolutions, peaceful or otherwise, necessarily mark ad-
vances; they may lead retreats as well. To think that
every change is a sign of progress is to commit what I
have named the fallacy of *post ergo melior.*

Ever since the Greeks of the fourth century B.C. discovered the distinction between natural law and man-
made or positive law, and even more intensively since
the discovery of experimental science in the seventeenth
century, men have dreamed of finding laws of society
which would be as firmly rooted as the laws of nature.
The Greeks meant by natural law not what that phrase
has since come to mean but rather the necessary principles of a successful society. Unfortunately, men have
often believed that they have found such laws, and they
have backed up their claims with ontological justifica-
tions, usually of a theological variety, through the possession of a divinely inspired absolute truth. There may
or may not be a god—I am not concerned with that
question here—but the fact is that the absolute truths
of the "world" religions do differ widely. And the com-
ing of cultural secularism has not altered that situation

materially; secular truths may be held just as absolutely and indeed often are, as is the case with Marxism. Indeed, there is nothing in the world cheaper or more prevalent than the absolute truth. Everybody has one.

No social laws can be held absolute in any final sense until all men agree as to their nature and establish them as the laws of a global society. In the meanwhile, the best of viable ideals is to suppose that every society has laws which are natural to it, given its ingredients and circumstances, and that natural laws applied in each case would give the same results as those which already prevail. But this conclusion serves only to reinforce the existing state of affairs, which must be wrong because of the fact of change. And so we are nowhere, unless we preserve the distinction made in the first instance between natural law and positive law.

Justice at the level of positive law is in the charge of the state and subject to it. But the fact that justice applies to the state as well as to those laws which were established by the state is evidence for the belief in the universal ideal of justice at the level of natural law. That is why revolutions to overthrow the state may come in the name of a wider justice than the state administers, even though it may happen that the revolution reduces rather than restores the level of justice. For Hans Kelsen, natural-law theories have operated to justify the forces of conservatism and reaction, while for Max Weber they have served to defend change and revolution. But unless there is justice at the level of natural law, there would be no protection of the individual's rights against incursion by the state.

What I am proposing, I suppose, is a modification and combination of the two traditional theories, which are usually conceived as opposed: natural-law theory and positive-law theory. Natural law, which is contained in the ideal of justice, becomes embodied in positive law, which is framed as an approach to it. Positive law reflects the expedient or short-range interests, natural law the long-range. Both serve the needs of the community; the former keeps it going, the latter keeps it on course. Positive law is contained in the organization of society as the morality directing its aims. This is what I have called ideal justice, with actual justice containing the direction toward the ideal.

A definition of social justice as the demand for order embodied in a system of laws places outside the state such capricious making and unmaking of the laws as occur when an arbitrary sovereign or absolute dictator rules by decree. There can be an order under such circumstances, but there is no system of order. The Constitution of 1936 of the Soviet Union laid down certain individual rights, but these have since been abrogated by the state, and there is no legal machinery for their remedy. A system of laws implies a greater comprehensiveness and a greater degree of permanence. Systems of order have to be forged under the trials of experience and of those modifications which time calls for.

The fact is that lawmakers do not operate in a vacuum or impulsively *de novo* but in strict accordance with the morality which exists in the society and by which it must be regulated. They are morality-codifiers proceeding in terms of legal interests. The law essentially means accepting restrictions on individual freedom as the vehicle of accommodation with others. There are, from time to time, changes in the morality of the society which call for corresponding changes in the law—for instance, the recognition of the right of privacy and the partial granting of legal rights to women in the latter part of the nineteenth century.

The principle of justice as the demand for order as embodied in a legal system has unlimited application to societies. And because systems are characterized by consistency and completeness, we should expect to find efforts made to see that these requirements are met. It is possible to read the judge-made law which exists in the citing of precedents as evidence that the legal system reaches for consistency. And when the laws are extended to include areas formerly left relatively free for individual action, such as labor laws, laws regulating insurance, and laws concerning the issuance of securities, it is possible to see the legal system reaching for completeness.

It might be added parenthetically that the ideal of a perfect legal theory is one which would be in such complete equilibrium with its society that there would be no infractions and so it would not be needed. At this point, order could become one with anarchy—only it would have to be a perfect order and a total anarchy. There is little danger that either will ever be attained.

Finally, the question inevitably arises (it certainly will in this case): Of what use is the theory of justice that I have been propounding in the foregoing pages? To this I can make two answers, one theoretical and one practical.

On the theoretical side my answer can be summed up in a single theorem: there is no useless knowledge. Once a truth has been discovered, it is only a matter of time before some application is found for it.

On the practical side I can make an answer in terms of more immediate relevance. From many quarters just now there is heard the demand for a thorough overhauling of the courts and the laws. How could this be accomplished without recourse to some comprehensive underlying principle? I submit that my definition of justice is a candidate for that position and, moreover, one that is peculiarly appropriate.

NOTES

I. THE CONCEPT OF JUSTICE
AND THE LAWS OF WAR

1. Rawls, A Theory of Justice (1971), hereafter cited as Rawls.
2. Rawls at 14.
3. Friedmann, *A Theory of Justice: A Lawyer's Critique*, 11 Colum. J. Transnat. Law 369, 374–76 (1972).
4. Rawls at 377–82.
5. *Id.* at 378–79.
6. Friedmann, *supra* note 3 at 378–79.
7. Rawls at 8.
8. Cf. Rousseau, The Social Contract, Bk. II, ch. III: "It is therefore essential, if the general will is able to express itself, that there should be no particularity within the State and that each citizen should think only his own thoughts."

9. Cf. Rawls at 13.
10. 4 Wheat. 316, 363 (1819).
11. *Id.* at 377.
12. *Id.* at 404–5.
13. J. L. Brierly, The Law of Nations (6th ed. 1963), cited by Rawls at 378, with the comment: "This work contains all that we need here." It is more than a little curious that Rawls invokes Brierly, who had less than no respect for the contract theory of justice. See Brierly, Basis of Obligation in International Law 16 (1958).
14. Brierly, Basis of Obligation, at 56.
15. Rawls at 378–79.
16. *Id.* at 379–82.
17. Brierly, Basis of Obligation, at 48.
18. See generally M. H. Keen, The Laws of War in the Late Middle Ages 7–22 (1965).
19. Eppstein, The Catholic Tradition of the Law of Nations 103 (1935). The writings of the Jesuit Francisco Suarez (1548–1617) are to the same effect.
20. Rawls at 378–79.
21. *Id.* at 379.
22. Taylor, Nuremberg and Vietnam: An American Tragedy 39–41 (1970).
23. See, e.g., Chomsky, *The Rule of Force in International Affairs*, 80 Yale L. J. 1456 (1971); Cohen, *Taylor's Conception of the Laws of War*, 80 Yale L. J. 1492 (1971); Wasserstrom, *Criminal Behavior*, N.Y. Review of Books 8–13 (June 3, 1971).
24. Wasserstrom, *supra* note 23 at 13.
25. Charles Francis Adams so described the point in his address "War Is Hell," delivered on January 26, 1903 in New York City at the thirteenth annual dinner, in

honor of Robert E. Lee, of the Confederate Veterans'
Camp of New York.

26. Brierly, *The Laws of War* in The Background and Issues of the War 130, n. 1 (1940), paraphrasing E. D.
Dickinson. Students and other auditors of talks I have
given on this subject have often made this point in
questions from the floor.

27. Brierly, *supra* note 26 at 130–31.

28. Rawls at 379.

29. XI Trials of War Criminals before the Nuremberg
Military Tribunals 1246–47.

30. Lieber Code LXVII. The Code has often been re-
printed, perhaps most recently in I The Law of War—
A Documentary History 158–86 (L. Friedman ed.
1972).

31. The Rawls point of view was, however, vigorously
advocated by the North Vietnamese government as
justifying the treatment of captured American flyers
as war criminals. See Taylor, *Defining War Crimes*,
N.Y. Times (Jan. 11, 1973) at 39.

32. See *supra* note 23.

33. Wasserstrom, *supra* note 23 at 12. See also Cohen, *supra*
note 23 at 1495.

34. Pollock & Maitland, History of English Law xxiii (2d
ed. 1899).

35. Brierly, The Laws of War, at 135–36.

36. Wasserstrom, *supra* note 23 at 13.

37. Taylor, Nuremberg and Vietnam, at 37–38.

38. Once again, Professor Wasserstrom misstated and over-
stated my position in interpreting it to mean that
"something ceases to be a war crime if both sides engage in the practice."

39. The Israeli tribunal that tried Adolf Eichmann was

practically though not nominally a "victor's" tribunal trying a captured "enemy."

40. Rawls at 236.

41. These conventions and many other documents relating to the laws of war are collected in The Law of War, *supra* note 30.

42. The lack of such provisions is, of course, immediately relevant to charges of war criminality against those responsible for or participating in the American aerial bombardments of North Vietnam.

43. Taylor, Nuremberg and Vietnam, at 140–43.

44. See the draft Hague Convention on the Rules of Air Warfare, reported in The Law of War, *supra* note 30 at 437–49.

45. See, e.g., Talleyrand's letter to Napoleon I, dated Nov. 20, 1806, quoted in part in The Law of War at xiv and set forth in translation in Woolsey, Introduction to the Study of International Law 306 (1st ed. 1860).

46. The court-martial proceedings against General Smith and others are reproduced in part in The Law of War, at 799–841.

47. The so-called "Leipzig trials" of 1921–22 are described in many works, including Taylor, Nuremberg and Vietnam, at 24. See also The Law of War, at 842–82.

48. The portions of this paper dealing with the Calley case were written many months prior to the events of 1974, when Calley's sentence was reduced to ten years and he was jailed to serve the remainder, subject to federal judicial review in proceedings which were still pending when this volume went to press.

49. Here, too, subsequent events have overtaken the text. In 1974 most of the Pakistani prisoners held in India were repatriated, and there appears to be little prospect of war-crimes proceedings against any of them.

II. CRIMINAL LAW:
"LAW AND ORDER" AND
THE CRIMINAL JUSTICE SYSTEM

1. New York Times, Jan. 26, 1973, at 18, col. 1.
2. See, e.g., New York State Senate Bill No. 1365 (identical to N.Y. Assembly Bill No. 1556), which was described by Governor Rockefeller in a speech before the New York State Legislature on January 3, 1973. The proposal contained harsh mandatory sentences for certain drug offenses and, in § 3 of the bill, made certain drug offenders ineligible for parole. On April 13, 1973, the governor announced that he was modifying the proposed bill to permit parole even in cases of mandatory life sentences after a required minimum period of imprisonment. The mandatory period would vary with the degree of the offense.
3. New York State Senate Bill No. 1365, §§ 12–13. Governor Rockefeller also modified this approach in his message of April 13, 1973.
4. See, generally, M. Frankel, Criminal Sentences (1972); Kadish, *Legal Norm and Discretion in the Police and Sentencing Processes*, 75 Harv. L. Rev. 904, 916 (1962).
5. Governor Rockefeller recently amended his proposal to extend minimum mandatory penalties to other crimes, including arson, burglary, rape, and robbery.
6. S. Rubin, H. Weihofen, G. Edwards & S. Rosenzweig, The Law of Criminal Correction 132 (1963); McCleery, *Authoritarianism and the Belief Systems of Incorrigibles*, in The Prison 260, 268–69 (D. Cressey ed. 1961); Kirby, *Doubts about the Indeterminate Sentence*, 53 Judicature 63 (1969).

7. See Frankel, *supra* note 4; Amsterdam, *The Supreme Court and the Rights of Suspects in Criminal Cases*, 45 N.Y.U.L. Rev. 785 (1970); Kadish, *supra* note 4.

8. New York State Judge Irwin Brownstein recently sentenced two youths to a life sentence with a mandatory minimum of fifteen years for acting as carriers of a quantity of heroin. As Judge Brownstein pointed out in a public statement, if the quantity had been just a little less, he could have given the defendants a lesser sentence, as he desired to do, since the defendants claimed that they did not know what was in the package.

9. U.S. Justice Dept., F.B.I., Uniform Crime Reports (1971). Of the 2,928,865 offenses reported during 1971 and included in the Reports, 574,584 (19 percent) were cleared (a crime is cleared when the police identify the offender, have sufficient evidence to charge him, and take him into custody). Considering the offenses indexed during 1971, 141,726 (4.8 percent of all index offenses reported) persons were found guilty as charged.

10. See, generally, Adams v. Williams, 407 U.S. 143 (1972); Chimel v. California, 395 U.S. 752 (1969); Terry v. Ohio, 392 U.S. 1 (1968); Draper v. United States, 358 U.S. 307 (1959).

11. 403 U.S. 573 (1971).

12. *Id.* at 574.

13. LaFave, Arrest—The Decision to Take a Suspect into Custody 63 (1965); Goldstein, *Police Discretion Not to Invoke the Criminal Process: Low Visibility Decisions in the Administration of Justice*, 69 Yale L.J. 543, 547 (1960); Kadish, *supra* note 4; Parnas, *Police Discretion and Diversion of Incidents of Intra-Family Violence*, 36 Law and Contemporary Problems 539 (1971).

14. Parnas, *supra* note 13.
15. United States Attorney's Office, Southern District of New York, Criminal Division Memo. No. 9 (Jan. 29, 1973), superseding in part Memo. No. 2, dated April 26, 1971 (available in the offices of the J. Crim. L. & C.).
16. Probation Manual, ch. 9, PO-9.11 (Dec. 1, 1961).
17. Judicial Conference of the United States, Report of the Committee on Probation, with Special Reference to Juvenile Delinquency (Aug. 21, 1947).
18. *Id.* at 7.
19. The President's Commission on Law Enforcement and Administration of Justice—Task Force Report: The Courts 7 (1967).
20. Bail Reform Act, 18 U.S.C. §§ 3146–52 (1971).
21. *Id.* at § 3146(b) (1971).
22. See note 2 *supra*.
23. See, generally, D. Newman, Conviction—The Determination of Guilt or Innocence without Trial (1966); Alschuler, *The Prosecutor's Role in Plea Bargaining*, 36 U. Chi. L. Rev. 50, 54 (1968); Note, *Influence of the Defendant's Plea on Judicial Determination of Sentence*, 66 Yale L.J. 204 (1956).
24. Fed. R. Crim. P. Rule 32(a); Cal. Penal Code § 1193 (West 1970); Ill. Rev. Stat. ch. 38, § 1005-5-3 (1973).
25. D. Newman, *supra* note 23 at 188–92; Lambros, *Plea Bargaining and the Sentencing Process*, 53 F.R.D. 509, 513 (1971); Comment, *Official Inducements to Plead Guilty: Suggested Morals for a Marketplace*, 32 U. Chi. L. Rev. 167 (1962).
26. Fed. R. Crim. P. Rule 37.
27. United States v. Marchese, 438 F.2d 452, 455 (2d Cir.), *cert. denied*, 402 U.S. 1012 (1971). The Court quoted Horning v. District of Columbia, 254 U.S. 135, 138 (1920).

28. Comprehensive Drug Abuse Prevention and Control Act of 1970, 21 U.S.C. § 841(a) (1972).

29. 18 U.S.C.A. § 4202 (1969).

30. Comprehensive Drug Abuse Prevention and Control Act of 1970, 21 U.S.C. § 841(a) (1972).

31. S.800, *as amended*, 93d Cong., 1st Sess., § 601 (1973), reproduced at 119 Cong. Rec. S6565 (1973).

32. Comprehensive Drug Abuse Prevention and Control Act of 1970, 21 U.S.C. § 841 (1972).

33. Opium Poppy Control Act of 1942, ch. 720, § 13, 56 Stat. 1045.

34. 119 Cong. Rec. S6549 (1973) (Remarks of Senator Ervin).

35. See Frankel, *supra* note 4.

36. Fed. R. Crim. P. Rule 32(c)(2).

37. Report of the National Institute for Law Enforcement and Criminal Justice, as summarized in "Southern District of New York Sentencing Study" at 3–4 (memorandum from United States Attorney, Southern District of New York, to Judges of the Second Circuit and Southern District of New York, mimeograph dated Jan. 10, 1973) (available from the offices of the J. Crim. L. & C.).

38. Statistical Report for Fiscal Year 1970, as quoted in "Southern District of New York Sentencing Study," *supra* note 37.

39. "Southern District of New York Sentencing Study," *supra* note 37.

40. 312 F. Supp. 863 (S.D.N.Y. 1970), *aff'd., modified, and rev'd* in part *sub. nom.*, Sostre v. McGinnis, 442 F.2d 178 (2d Cir. 1971) (En banc), *cert. denied*, 404 U.S. 1049 (1972).

41. 340 F.Supp. 544 (W.D. Wis. 1972), *rev'd and remanded*, 489 F.2d 1335 (7th Cir. 1973).

42. 312 F. Supp. at 869.
43. *Id.* at 871.
44. Correction Law § 140 (McKinney 1970).
45. Correction Law § 137 (McKinney 1972).
46. Sostre v. McGinnis, 442 F.2d 178, 198 (2d Cir. 1971) (En banc), *cert. denied.*, 404 U.S. 1049 (1972).
47. 312 F. Supp. at 868.
48. Morales v. Schmidt, 340 F. Supp. 544, 548–49 (W.D. Wis. 1972), *rev'd and remanded,* 489 F.2d 1335 (7th Cir. 1973).
49. Functions of the United States Board of Parole 4–5 (1964).
50. Frankel, *supra* note 4 at 106.
51. 18 U.S.C. § 4209 (1969).
52. Federal Youth Correction Act, 18 U.S.C. §§ 5005–26 (1970).
53. Frankel, *supra* note 4 at 21.
54. Frankel, *supra* note 4. For other sentencing proposals, see Am. B. Ass'n Project on Minimum Standards for Justice: Standards Relating to Sentencing Alternatives (1968); National Council on Crime and Delinquency, Model Sentencing Act (1963).
55. Frankel, *supra* note 4 at 113.
56. *Id.* at 114.

III. PHILOSOPHICAL PERSPECTIVES ON JUSTICE

1. Gorgias, 484D–E.
2. Theaetetus, 172C.
3. *Id.* at 172D–E.
4. I am aware of the arguments of those who insist that a definition of justice is not required (Bodenheimer) and

that to attempt one would be futile (Lask). For the former see Edgar Bodenheimer, Treatise on Justice 262 (1967); for the latter see The Legal Philosophies of Lask, Radbruch, and Dabin 21 (Kurt Wilk trans. 1950).

5. Critique of Pure Reason, A 656; B 684.

6. See, e.g., Brian Gardner, The East India Company (1972).

7. V Collected Papers of Charles Sanders Peirce pars. 450, 505 ff. (C. Hartshorne and P. Weiss eds. 1960).

8. "Due process is that which comports with the deepest notions of what is fair and right and just. The more fundamental the beliefs are the less likely they are to be explicitly stated. But respect for them is of the very essence of the due process clause. In enforcing them this Court does not translate personal views into constitutional limitations. In applying such a large, untechnical concept as 'due process,' the Court enforces those permanent and pervasive feelings of our society as to which there is compelling evidence of the kind relevant to judgments of our social institutions." Mr. Justice Frankfurter in his dissenting opinion in Solesbee v. Balkcom, 339 U.S. 9, 16 (1950). Again, "the difficulties are inherent not only in the nature of words, of composition, and of legislation generally. They are often intensified by the subject matter of an enactment. The imagination which can draw an income tax statute to cover the myriad transactions of a society like ours, capable of producing the necessary revenue without producing a flood of litigation, has not yet revealed itself." 1 Report of Income Tax Codification Committee, Cmd. 5131, 16–19 (1936). Moreover, government sometimes solves problems by temporarily shelving them. Felix Frankfurter, Some Reflections on the Reading of Statutes: The Sixth Annual Benjamin N. Cardozo

Lecture 7 (1947). The legislative process reflects that attitude. Statutes as well as constitutional provisions at times embody purposeful ambiguity or are expressed with a generality for future unfolding. The prohibition contained in the Fifth Amendment refers to "infamous crimes"—a term obviously inviting interpretation in harmony with conditions and opinions prevailing from time to time. Cf. Mr. Justice Brandeis in United States v. Moreland, 258 U.S. 433, 451. As Mr. Justice Cardozo once remarked, a great principle of constitutional law is not susceptible of comprehensive statement in an adjective. Carter v. Carter Coal Co., 298 U.S. 238, 327.

9. Law of the Constitution 202 (9th ed., Wade ed.).

10. Huntington Cairns, The Theory of Legal Science 1 (1941).

11. *Disorder*, in The Concept of Order 3–13 (Kuntz ed. 1968).

12. Examples in modern history are not hard to find. The United States wrested Texas from Mexico. The Soviet Union overran the Baltic States—Latvia, Lithuania, and Estonia—and invaded Hungary and Czechoslovakia. Communist China seized Tibet.

13. 336B–354C.

14. 482C–486E.

15. The idea that justice is not confined to the human domain is as old as Anaximander (ca. B.C. 560), who wrote that "the source from which existing things derive their existence is also that to which they return at their destruction, according to necessity; for they give justice and make reparation to one another for their injustice, according to the arrangement of Time." Kathleen Freeman, Ancilla to the Pre-Socratic Philosophers 19 (1948). Although it is obvious that in what follows I shall be talking about justice as it exists in human

society and material culture, it is the abstract idea of justice, with a wider interpretation, that is still assumed in the background.

16. That there can be a proper fitting of parts in wholes in domains other than that of the human species is amply illustrated by plate tectonics in geology.

17. The same thing can be said of law that was said of justice: "Over thousands of years the most powerful minds of all nations have been unable to agree on a universal definition of law." W. Friedmann, Legal Theory 421 (1949).

18. Morris R. Cohen observed that "though the law may never become a completely logical system, it can never entirely dispense with the effort in that direction." Reason and Law (Prologue). Those laws on which the state rests are axiomatic and are usually framed in a constitution or charter, written or unwritten.

19. In the sense that it is by means of a system of laws that justice is effected in human society, justice is prior to law. But in the empirical sense of the exigencies of society, justice is not the source of the law, as some have claimed. It was the medieval idea of law that justice is the source of law. See, e.g., Walter Ullmann, The Medieval Idea of Law: As Represented by Lucas de Penna (1946), esp. ch. III.

20. In mathematics a consistent system is one which does not contain any contradictions, and a complete system is one in which every true sentence is a theorem. One of the favorite ways of proving the consistency of a mathematical system is to make a model of it; and when such a model consists in a concrete interpretation, as it so often does, the procedure implies the assumption of the consistency of the material universe.

21. More specifically, in mathematics these are called "ob-

jects"; and "structure-preserving functions," called "mappings or morphisms," are preserved between them. Cf. William S. Hatcher, Foundations of Mathematics ch. 8, sec. 1, esp. p. 267 (1968).

22. Eth. Nic., 1131b18.
23. In mathematics a set of elements is said to be partially ordered with respect to a relation R if R is reflexive, antisymmetric, and transitive.
24. Moral Strategy 131 (1967).
25. The Reach of Politics 61 (1969).
26. Republic, VI, 509.
27. Arnold J. Toynbee, V A Study of History 29ff. (1935).
28. There is a considerable body of argument for justice as part of morality in Aristotle. See esp. Eth. Nic., bk. V.
29. New York Times, Jan. 9, 1972, at 1.
30. *Id.* at 24.
31. Cf. Paul L. Murphy, The Constitution in Crisis Times: 1918–1969 (1972).

PUBLISHED ROSENTHAL
LECTURES 1948–1973

1948   Hazard, John N. "The Soviet Union and International Law," *Illinois Law Review*, XLIII, 591.

1949   Freund, Paul A. *On Understanding the Supreme Court*. Boston: Little, Brown & Co.

1951   Dawson, John P. *Unjust Enrichment, A Comparative Analysis*. Boston: Little, Brown & Co.

1952   Feller, Abraham H. *United Nations and World Community*. Boston: Little, Brown & Co.

1952   Horsky, Charles A. *The Washington Lawyer*. Boston: Little, Brown & Co.

1953   Vanderbilt, Arthur T. "The Essentials of a Sound Judicial System," *Northwestern University Law Review*, XLVIII.

1954   Berle, Adolf A., Jr. *The Twentieth Century Capitalist Revolution*. New York: Harcourt, Brace.

1956   Hurst, James W. *Law and the Conditions of Freedom in the Nineteenth Century United States*. Madison: University of Wisconsin Press.

1956 Sohn, Louis B. "United Nations Charter Revision and the Rule of Law: A Program for Peace," *Northwestern University Law Review*, L, 709.

1956 Gross, Ernest A. "Major Problems in Disarmament," *Northwestern University Law Review*, LI, 299.

1956 Parker, John J. "Dual Sovereignty and the Federal Courts," *Northwestern University Law Review*, LI, 407.

1957 Ukai, Nobushige. "The Individual and the Rule of Law Under the New Japanese Constitution," *Northwestern University Law Review*, LI, 733.

1957 Papale, Antonia Edward. "Judicial Enforcement of Desegregation: Its Problems and Limitations," *Northwestern University Law Review*, LII, 301.

1957 Hart, Herbert L. A. "Murder and the Principles of Punishment: England and the United States," *Northwestern University Law Review*, LII, 433.

1958 Green, Leon. *Traffic Victims: Tort Law and Insurance*. Evanston, Ill.: Northwestern University Press.

1960 Radcliffe, Cyril John. *The Law and Its Compass*. Evanston, Ill.: Northwestern University Press.

1961 Eisenstein, Louis. *The Ideologies of Taxation*. New York: Ronald Press.

1961 Havighurst, Harold C. *The Nature of Private Contract*. Evanston, Ill.: Northwestern University Press.

1962 Pike, James Albert. *Beyond the Law: The Religious and Ethical Meaning of the Lawyer's Vocation*. New York: Doubleday & Co.

1964   Katz, Wilber G. *Religion and American Constitutions*. Evanston, Ill.: Northwestern University Press.

1965   Cowen, Zelman. *The British Commonwealth of Nations in a Changing World: Law, Politics, and Prospects*. Evanston, Ill.: Northwestern University Press.

1967   Schaefer, Walter V. *The Suspect and Society: Criminal Procedure and Converging Constitutional Doctrines*. Evanston, Ill.: Northwestern University Press.

1967   Freedman, Max, Beaney, William M., and Rostow, Eugene V. *Perspectives on the Court*. Evanston, Ill.: Northwestern University Press.

1968   Donner, André M. *The Role of the Lawyer in the European Communities*. Evanston, Ill.: Northwestern University Press.

1969   McGowan, Carl. *The Organization of Judicial Power in the United States*. Evanston, Ill.: Northwestern University Press.

1969   Jones, Harry W. *The Efficacy of Law*. Evanston, Ill.: Northwestern University Press.

1971   Goldberg, Arthur J. *Equal Justice: The Warren Era of the Supreme Court*. Evanston, Ill.: Northwestern University Press.

1973   Taylor, Telford, Motley, Constance Baker, and Feibleman, James K. *Perspectives on Justice*. Evanston, Ill.: Northwestern University Press.

A NOTE ON MANUFACTURE

THE TEXT OF THIS BOOK was set on the Linotype in a face
called JANSON, an "Old Face" of the Dutch school cut in
Amsterdam by the Hungarian, Nickolas Kis, *circa* 1690.
Janson's authorship was long attributed erroneously to
Anton Janson, a Hollander who had been employed in
Leipzig where the matrices were rediscovered. These
same mats are today in the possession of the Stempel
foundry, Frankfurt, and the machine-cast version you
are reading was modelled directly on type produced
from the original strikes.

The book was composed, printed, and bound by
KINGSPORT PRESS, INC., Kingsport, Tennessee. WARREN
PAPER COMPANY manufactured the paper. The typog-
raphy and binding designs are by *Guy Fleming*.